THE LANDSCAPES
PAINTING BOOK

in watercolor
and oils

THE LANDSCAPES
PAINTING BOOK

in watercolor
and oils

José M. Parramón

**The art of landscape painting
in oils and watercolor: origins and
development, materials and techniques,
themes, composition and interpretation,
color theories and practical
step by step exercises.**

Fig. 2. Vicenç Ballestar. *The River* (detail). **Private collection. Ballestar demonstrates how to paint this watercolor step by step on pages 144 to 147.**

Director: José Mª. Parramón Vilasaló
Text: José Mª. Parramón Vilasaló
Edition, layout and proofs: José Mª. Parramón Vilasaló
Photography: Nos y Soto

Translated from the Spanish by Monica Krüger

© José Mª Parramón Vilasaló

ISBN 84-95323-11-7

Photosetting and photocromes: Novasis, S.A.L.
Printed in Spain

Table of Contents

Fig. 3 (opposite page). José M. Parramón (b. 1919). *Wheat field with Breda in the background* (detail). Private collection. You can see this painting in figure 365 on page 137.

To my dear wife, María

Table of Contents

4

4A

4B

Fig. 4. José M. Parramón. *Mountain Refuge*
(50 x 55 cm). Private collection. To paint this
watercolor I started with an on the spot
sketch of the scene to study the subject's
potential (fig. 4A). Next, as always, I took
a photo (fig. 4B) and finally I painted the
watercolor in the studio using the sketch
and the photo as references.

Introduction

Discussing how to paint landscape and its development by studying the techniques and styles of the impressionists and Post-Impressionists such as Monet, Cézanne, Van Gogh and watercolorists such as Turner, Homer and Sargent may seem an old fashioned method, somewhat out of place with current forward thinking attitudes.

However, read what Robert Hughes has to say on the subject, art critic of The Times 25 years ago and considered "the most controversial critic in the United States and, in all honesty, the most sincere" according to the reporter Martínez de Pisón. Hughes. In an interview with this reporter, he claimed that "Today's art schools have become creches whose pupils have no knowledge of the creators of modern art; Dégas, Matisse, Picasso, Miró, Mondrian, De Koning, etc. who had studied in the way of the old school and who were in the practice of making figure studies and drawing from nature". And later he added, "If you compare the end of this century to the end of the last, our current artists are neither as numerous nor of such stature as Cézanne, Monet, Seurat, Van Gogh, Gauguin, Dégas, Matisse, Munch or Rodin".

This issue does not arise when it comes to watercolor landscape painting, there is no avant garde: all the recognised painters in this field today, whether in Europe or America, paint with a style that is closer to impressionism than any other genre.

Learning to paint landscapes in oils or in watercolor using the techniques and following the example of the masters of Impressionism, Postimpressionism and Fauvism is the correct approach. It works so effectively that practically everybody, art students and professional artists world-wide, paint landscapes with Monet, Cézanne, Pissarro Renoir, Sisley etc. in mind. They aim at times to remind us of Van Gogh or Gauguin, occasionally echoing Matisse and the fauves. What it comes down to is that these painters' ways of expression are what appeals, what is accepted, enjoyed and bought by most of today's art buyers.

This book is written with these concepts in mind; looking first at a collection of masterpieces, starting with watercolor works by Dürer and the first pure landscape paintings, in oils, by the Dutch, up until Picasso's landscapes. This chapter is followed by one on materials and tools, techniques and skills needed for oil painting and watercolor. We then progress onto studying the principles of drawing and painting landscapes, the rules of perspective, sketches, how to calculate dimension and proportion, choosing your subject matter, a well equipped studio such as one used by Monet or Turner; and a series of lessons and useful tips on how to compose and interpret the subject. One of the chapters focuses on the study of the components of landscape such as skies, earth/the ground, shadows, the sea, figures etc., another looks at color theory, color harmonies and color ranges, tonalist and colorist approaches and finishing up with practical exercises painting landscapes in watercolor and oils, through the step by step development of pictures painted especially for this book.

José M. Parramón

5

Fig. 5. José M. Parramón, author of this book on landscape and of thirty eight other books on the study of drawing and painting, translated and published in fourteen countries, including the United States, Russia and Japan.

6

Fig. 6. Paul Cézanne (1839-1906). *The bay of Marseilles seen from L'Estaque* (detail). Musée d'Orsay, Paris. This subject was painted many times by Cézanne who would slightly alter the viewpoint and the format, but always included the little fishermen's village of L'Estaque with the bay in the background.

A GALLERY OF
LANDSCAPE
PAINTING HISTORY

More of a picture gallery than a history lesson, this is no
attempt at an in-depth study, it is simply a visual résumé
of major works providing information on the development of the landscape genre in oils and watercolors.
Explanations help you appreciate each picture, with
schematic drawings and commentaries, and the interpretation of subject and color schemes. In these first few
pages this history will help you understand what and how
the great masters painted and how they approached the
task of painting these magnificent landscapes.

Introduction to the Genre

Landscape, or what we in the West understand as *landscape* –a drawing or painting whose main theme is the representation of a natural or urban scene–, did not appear until Albrecht Dürer painted a series of watercolors in Germany at the end of the fifteenth century. The landscape genre appears as a more official and recognised genre, at the beginnings of the sixteenth century in the Low Countries, at the beginnings of Holland's independence. One detail that must be clarified is that landscape as the background of figure paintings has been a regular feature in paintings, specially from the Renaissance onwards. It should also be remembered that in the Far East, watercolor landscape painters were already painting in the eighth century. But let us look at this in phases.

In ancient Greece, 400 years before Christ, landscapes were already being painted, but these always served as a background for mythological scenes in which the figure was the principal theme. In Roman painting we see depictions of landscapes decorating walls but they fall under the category called "third style, ornamental", but both their size and their indecisiveness make it evident that they were nothing more than simple vignettes (fig. 7).

After this... a void. During the Gothic period and the Renaissance, landscape always appeared as a complementary background; there were even artists who specialized in executing this part of the painting. To illustrate this, an extract from a Perugian artist's contract says "...whose undertaking is to paint landscapes and cloudscapes in the empty spaces behind the figures".

There were of course exceptions. Leonardo da Vinci (1452-1510) painted the landscapes featured in his figure paintings himself. What's more, he achieved this with his extraordinary combination of technical and artistic skill, illustrating how to paint atmospheric effects to suggest the different planes and to represent the third dimension or how to create contrasts to differentiate and separate masses from each other; two of the many effects that Leonardo de Vinci had discovered and discussed in his famous book, *Treatise on Painting* (figs. 8 & 9).

7

8

9

There were also figure painters, –we are still referring to the Renaissance here– who saw and painted landscape as something more than a mere complementary motif. The Venetian, Giorgio de Castelfranco, known as Il Giorgione (1476-1510) was one of these. In all of his outdoor figure paintings the composition pivoted on the predominant role of the landscape (fig. 10). This tendency can be seen most clearly in the painting called *The tempest*, considered as the first dramatic landscape (fig. 11) This is a painting in which Giorgione painted a true landscape although nobody to this day can explain what the two figures are doing or what they represent in a painting titled *The tempest*.

Fig. 7 (above). Unknown painter, Ancient Rome, *Sacred Landscape*. National Museum of Naples. Painted about ten years before the birth of Christ, during the reign of Emperor Augustus. Judging by its size and original position it is probably a decorative vignette which came from the Red Room of a Villa in Boscotrecase, near Pompeii and was probably inspired by a painting from the Ancient Greek period.

Fig. 10. Il Giorgione/Titian. *The pastoral concert*. Musée du Louvre. Paris. Historians have stated that the concept and composition are Titian's and that the work is painted by Il Giorgione. In any case it is an example of the presence of landscape emphasised by Il Giorgione, no longer a simple backdrop but an integral part of the painting.

Figs. 8 & 9 (opposite page). Leonardo da Vinci. *Leda*. Borghese Gallery, Rome. This painting is a copy of the original and is a work of one of Leonardo's pupils. The original has been lost, but the technique and the quality are proof that the original was painted by Leonardo da Vinci. In figure 8 (left) you can see a detail of the landscape which appears in the top left-hand corner of the picture.

Fig. 11. Giorgione. *The tempest*. The Academia, Venice. Il Giorgione's attempts to make landscape the main point of interest in his paintings is clearly evident in this painting, the first ambient/theatrical landscape painted in tempera in which the presence of the two enigmatic figures still cannot be explained.

Landscape in the Far East. China and Japan

In eighth century China during the T'ang Imperial dynasty (608-906), the tradition of painting landscapes on rolls of paper and silk began. Two hundred years later during the period called the Five Dynasties (906-960), landscape –called *shan-shui* (mountains and water)– was already being painted in full colour (fig. 12). During the following Imperial reign, the Sung Dynasty (960-1279), watercolor landscape was influenced by Buddhism and the religious doctrines of Zen philosophy; they used washes of black Chinese ink or sepia, overlaid with watercolor washes (fig. 13).

In the thirteenth century the indomitable Gengis Khan, his son and his nephew led the Mongols to conquer China, and the Yuan dynasty was created (1260-1368). However, the barbarous Mongols adopted and developed the artistic traditions of the Sung dynasty. A century later a revolution broke out which liberated China and founded the Ming dynasty.

Fig. 12. Unattributed painting from the Five Dynasties period (906-960). *Deer amongst red maples*, on vertically rolled silk, ink and watercolor.

Fig. 13 (below left). Attributed to the Emperor Hui-tsung. *Autumn in the hills and river*. Vertically rolled paper, ink and delicate watercolors. By courtesy of the National Palace and the Central Museum of the republic of China. The landscape carries the initials and the seal of the Emperor and painter Hui-tsung, who reigned from 1101 to 1125 during the Sung Dynasty.

Fig. 14 (below center). Ch'iu Ying, *Waiting for the autumn crossing boat*. Vertical roll from the Ming dynasty, ink and delicate watercolor. By courtesy of the National Palace and the Central Museum of the Republic of China.

Fig. 15 (opposite page). Utagawa Hiroshige. *Kandara*. Station number 16 in the series "Fifty three stations of Tokaido". Edo period. Fuji Museum, Tokyo.

Fig. 16 (opposite page). Utagawa Hiroshige. *Rainy night in Karasaki*. Musée Guimet, Paris. This is one of the most beautiful scenes of the series "Eight views of Omi", because of the way it creatively represents the rain as a curtain of vertical lines which lash down, enveloping the huge tree in a mist through which only the silhouette is visible.

Fig. 17 (opposite page). Katsushika Hokusai. *Mount Fuji visible amongst the Waves*, Fuji Museum, Tokyo. This painting belongs to the series "Fifty six views of Mount Fuji" which Hokusai painted between 1829 and 1831, this wave is the best known image of the series.

The artists of the Imperial Court of the Ming dynasty (1360-1644) did not produce any work of merit and it was at this time that landscape painting extended beyond the courts and was being practised in schools and centers including Chekiang and Wu-hsien where the so called Learned Ones, were painting a group who were influenced by the style of the Sung and Yuan dynasties (fig. 14).

In 1644 the Manchus occupied Peking and founded a new dynasty, the Ts'ing dynasty which governed China from 1644 to 1912, when it was proclaimed a republic. During this last Imperial dynasty the court artists came to the fore once more, they worked with a number of painters who came over from the West, painting more realistic landscapes introducing the use of shadow and shading. These "Learned Ones" expressed their preferences for Chinese landscape as painted by the artists of earlier times.

Documented history of Japan dates from 552 AD However, it was not until six hundred years later in the Kamakura period of the twelfth century (1185-1333), that the Japanese started painting landscapes. Initially they imitated the Chinese landscapes which arrived in Japan along with Zen philosophy. It was during the Muromachi period (1333-1573), that Japanese landscape reached its zenith, as the Japanese *yamato-e* style was developed (fig. 15). Following this time was the brief Momoyama period (1573-1614) which saw development of richer decorative details. Then came the Edo period (1614-1868), and the introduction of woodcut, which introduced a new style based on line drawing and flat planes of watercolor (fig. 16). This style also affected the interpretation of the subject which was perceived with a decorativism and synthesis far removed from the influences of Chinese landscape (fig. 17).

15

16

17

Albrecht Dürer, the First Landscape Painter

Dürer's father was a goldsmith and when he was twelve years old Albrecht left the Latin school of St Lawrence in Nuremberg and joined the workshop of his father as an apprentice. Michael Wolgemut, a famous painter and maker of etchings for books, lived very close to Dürer and the little boy would go over to Herr Wolgemut's house every single day. Wolgemut spoke with the boy's father saying "Your son will not work with gold as you do, he will not be a goldsmith, he will be a painter". But the father wanted his son to continue developing the business and to this end he rented a new workshop for five florins a year, near Nuremberg city hall.

Then an unexpected incident took place. The young Dürer, at only thirteen years old, drew the now famous self portrait which is currently in the Albertina Museum in Vienna. His father went to see Herr Wolgemut, "You are right" he said, "my son will not be a goldsmith. Look at this", and he showed him the self portrait (fig. 18).

18

Albrecht Dürer studied under Herr Wolgemut for three years, working on his extraordinary skills in drawing and painting and learning how to make etchings. Later he was to become the most famous maker of etchings in the whole of Europe.

Fig. 18. Albrecht Dürer (1471-1528). *Self portrait*, drawing. Albertina, Vienna. Dürer drew this self portrait when he was 13 years old. Years later an inscription was added in his handwriting which says "I drew this self portrait in front of a mirror in 1484, when I was just a boy. Albrecht Dürer".

Fig. 20. Albrecht Dürer. *View over Kalchreuth*, 1511, watercolor. On display in Bremen, Kunsthalle. Here is a landscape painted by Dürer nearly five hundred years ago which is comparable to watercolors painted today in terms of the crispness of the drawing and the application of paint.

2

Five years later, in 1494, after he was married Dürer visited Venice. A year later, on his return to Nuremberg, he travelled through the Italian Alps, crossing the Tyrol along the Adigio route and painted, from life in watercolor, the first pure landscapes in Western History of Art. Amongst them was the little village of Arco which you can see below (fig. 19).

Years later, in 1511, he painted the landscape View over Kalchreuth, a village near Nuremberg (fig. 20). Dürer painted eighty six watercolors in all, of which thirty were landscapes, but despite the evident quality of these watercolors, Dürer considered them nothing more than simple studies which, he said, "I could not honorably part with for money".

Fig. 19. Albrecht Dürer. *View of Arco*, 1495, Musée du Louvre, Paris. This is one of the greatest watercolors painted by Dürer during his return journey to Nuremberg, note the exquisite detail in the olive trees and vines, the town at the base of the enormous rocky outcrop and the walls and fortresses on the peak of the mountain.

19

The First Landscapes in Oils with Figures

In Antwerp in the spring of the year 1521 the Flemish artist Joachim Patenier was remarried. Amongst the guests was Albrecht Dürer, who, before returning to Nuremberg, made a lead pencil drawing of his friend Patenier. When the time came for Dürer to leave, Patenier wished to give Dürer one of his paintings and invited him to choose from a number of canvases.

"It is difficult to choose", said Dürer, "I like them all. I see that you have employed the manner of the Antwerp school: a foreground composed of browns, a middle ground of greens and background of blues. My congratulations to you, I have always claimed that you are surely the most skilled landscape painter in Flanders". "My thanks dear colleague", and Patenier added a remark, "As you know, some of these figures are not painted by me but by Metsys. Do you know him?". Yes, Dürer knew Metsys and he was not surprised that one or more small figures appeared in the foreground of all Patenier's landscapes. This was a tradition that continued up until the beginnings of the sixteenth century. However, Patenier invented his landscapes (fig. 21), while many other artists were painting landscapes directly from nature or from sketches drawn in situ, in front of the subject.

One of these subjects was the Alps, an obligatory passing point for Central and Northern European artists who would travel to Italy in order to see the artists of the Renaissance. The German, Albrecht Altdorfer (1480-1538) was one of those artists, initially a figure painter, he decided to travel to Italy along the river Danube and on passing through the Austrian Alps he was so overwhelmed by the landscapes he saw that he became a landscape painter (fig. 22). From this point onwards, figure painting held no

Fig. 21. Joachim Patenier. *Landscape with St Jerome.* **Museo del Prado, Madrid.** Patenier's landscapes are always fantastical and artificial, sometimes even illogical in their composition, a result of the rich imagination of an artist who worked without a model, inventing the features of each landscape.

Fig. 21A. Joachim Patenier was one of the first artists to apply a formula instigated by the mannerists of Antwerp; a foreground of browns, a middle ground of greens and a large panoramic background of blues.

Fig. 22. Albrecht Altdorfer. *Saint George in the wood.* **Old Pinacoteca, Munich.** Although the figure of Saint George appears in this landscape, it is to Altdorfer that the concept of pure landscape –landscape without figures– is attributed. He broke with the convention that a landscape painting had to tell a story.

Fig. 23 (opposite page). Pieter Bruegel the Elder. *Winter landscape with skaters and bird trap.* **Royal Art Museum of Belgium, Brussels.**

Fig. 24 (opposite page). Peter Paul Rubens. *Shepherd with his flock in a wooded landscape.* **National Gallery, London.**

interest for Altdorfer, "The whispering of the leaves on the trees by the lakeside at the foot of the mountains is the only subject that captivates me", he wrote in one of his letters.

Pieter Bruegel the Elder (1525/30-1569) is another example, except that he alternated between his now well known figure paintings with his remarkable landscape paintings (fig. 23). When he was twenty five, Bruegel made the trip to Italy, crossing the Alps whose natural splendour "created a tremendous impact on him, to such an extent that if you study his Alpine drawings it is evident that in his development up until this point, observe Art History experts Peter and Linda Murray.

Finally, Peter Paul Rubens (1577-1640) a master of the human figure in religious and mythological scenes also painted some impressive landscapes habitually including figures that lent a title to the painting (fig. 24).

23

24

Philip II, Calvin and the Introduction of

It was during the sixteenth century when Philip II, King of Spain and the Low Countries became aware of the teachings of a Friar called Calvin who was converting the people in the north of the Low Countries to Protestantism.

"And, what's more, they are asking for independence!", the Duke of Alba exclaimed furiously.

"Go there and subdue them!", the King ordered.

But the King had made an error. The Duke of Alba went to the northern part of the Low Countries just like the Attila's Horse. He raised taxes and suppressed the religious and political uprisings with such force that finally in 1581 the people declared their independence and proclaimed themselves the Republic of Holland. From this moment the Low Countries was divided into two nations; Flanders in the south was Catholic while Holland in the North was Protestant. This caused a development in the art world. While religious and mythological paintings continued to be produced in Flanders, the painters in Holland were producing art along more secular lines; group portraits, still lifes, interiors and landscapes.

Landscape, yes pure landscape; a theme inspired by their land, their climate and their Protestant religion, which banned the production of secular images. For this very reason the artists in Holland had their choices limited to secular images, including landscape, as subjects for their paintings.

If you study the following pages you will find images and text concerning five of the most famous Dutch artists of this period. Salomon van Ruysdael (1600-1670), was a painter of realist landscapes, he started painting very young and the subject matter and monochromatic palette –greens, yellows, earth colors and greys– of his early years is evidence that he was influenced by his friend the landscape artist Jan van Goyen. This similarity is particularly striking in the landscapes featuring a stretch of water with boats and trees on the shoreline (fig. 25). However, he soon broke away from this influence thanks to his nephew Jacob (figs. 26 and 26A).

Jacob van Ruysdael (1628/9-1682), a nephew of Salomon, was the most important painter of Dutch realist landscape. He received his initial training from his father and his uncle Salomon. Like the majority of Dutch artists he painted landscapes with low horizons and huge skies full of dense, dramatic cloud formations (figs. 27 and 27A). He skillfully alternated between a monochromatic palette and the use of intense, luminous color (fig. 28). He was also the teacher of Meindert Hobbema, who we will discuss in the following pages.

Fig. 25 (below). Salomon van Ruysdael. *Dutch Canal.* Maurithuis, The Hague. Cloudy sky, low horizon, a river or estuary to the sea with one or more ships, a town in the background and one or more trees to break up the monotony of the horizon line. A classic composition scheme seen in many of Salomon van Ruysdael's landscapes.

Fig. 26 (opposite page). *Sailing boats near a village.* Museo Thyssen Bornemisza, Madrid. This landscape, painted in 1660, is a clear example of the alteration in Salomon van Ruysdael's painting style from 1640 onwards; he uses a more diverse color range having been influenced by his nephew Jacob van Ruisdael.

Fig. 26A (opposite page). Given the wide chromatic range of this image it is not easy to determine a definite schematic. However, just take a look at the diagram which simplifies the colors and elements that make up Salomon van Ruysdael's landscape.

Fig. 27 (opposite page, right). Jacob van Ruysdael. *The windmill at Dordrecht.* Rijksmuseum, Amsterdam. A famous picture, Robert Genaill the critic explained why in the following comment "... The monumental harmonies created by the verticals and horizontals, the interplay between light and shade and the silvery echoes of the grey Rhine combine under the grey-blue skies".

25

Landscape painted in Oils by the Dutch

27

26A

27A

28A

28

Fig. 27A (right). The basic schematic of *The windmill of Dordrecht* consists of a horizontal and a diagonal created by the windmill and the intense clouds in the background behind and to the right of the windmill.

Fig. 28. Jacob van Ruysdael. *Road crossing fields of corn near Zuider Zee.* Museo Thyssen Bornemisza, Madrid. Jacob van Ruysdael puts his very soul into each of his landscapes. Seen here, next to landscapes such as *The windmill*, with the dramatic impact of a grey scene with stormy skies, Jacob paints a sky of vivid cumulus clouds and contrasts this with the ground highlighted with shards of sun which pick out the background and the shadows that throw the foreground details into deep shade making them hardly distinguishable.

Fig. 28A (above right). A horizontal format, giving generous space to the sky. Holland is a country of flat landscapes and cloudy skies, threatening storm clouds or cumulus clouds promising good weather is a recurring theme, appearing in the vast majority of Dutch landscapes.

Famous Dutch Landscapist of the Seventeenth Century

These artists became so famous and revered that until well into the nineteenth century there were many artists who adopted their style, painting landscapes which were reminiscent both in theme and composition to those of the Dutch Landscape artists. They were famous, but they suffered economic hardship because there had been such an upsurge in the painting market. Some of the most skilled artists –Hals, Vermeer, Salomon van Ruysdael and Hobbema– suffered as the market degenerated into a ferocious competition ground. Hobbema was married at the age of thirty and had to become a tax collector in order to make money, deserting his painting for twenty years.

Rembrandt van Rijn (1606-1669) was fifty on 20 of July, 1656. His debts were so substantial that the Supreme Court of Amsterdam ordered the take over and sale of all his assets, including his sizeable collection of paintings, amongst which were seventy of his own, eight of the Landscape artist

Seghers, two albums "with landscapes drawn from nature by Rembrandt" and nine paintings of "landscapes drawn from nature by the same artist". The Stone Bridge was one of these nine landscapes (figs. 29 & 29A). Painted in 1637 or thereabouts, you can see how Rembrandt highlighted only one part of the subject, concentrating the light on the trees in the center and on the profile of the bridge. The rest of the canvas is left in deep shadow and chiaroscuro, similar to the format that he used for his portrait paintings. Also notice how Rembrandt follows the guidelines for Dutch landscape here, lowering the horizon to occupy one third of the picture plane giving over two thirds to the storm-ridden cloudy sky.

Meindert Hobbema (1638-1709) is another of the great Dutch landscape painters. Friend and pupil of Jacob van Ruysdael, he went out to paint with his master from a very early age, which is why there is some dispute over paintings, as it is sometimes hard to distinguish between their work. His

first paintings date from 1658. At 20 years old he was already a well recognised painter. Take a look at the picture opposite (fig. 30), painted in 1660 when he was 22 years old. It is regrettable that at the age of thirty and recently married, he was employed by the city council of Amsterdam and practically stopped painting altogether, because when you study The Avenue at Middelharnis (fig. 31), painted in 1689 when he was 51, you can see a clear evolution of his skills and admire the quality of this later work. Finally, Albert Cuyp (1620-1691), landscape and seascape painter, is another of the great artists of the time, comparable to those we have just discussed, this is evident in the Seascape, *The mass at Dordrecht* (fig. 32). As well as landscapes, Albert Cuyp painted portraits, still lifes and animals which he included on a small scale into his landscapes. Another characteristic of his art is the range of warm colors and golden atmospheric effects that he used, inspired by the celebrated paintings of Claude Lorrain.

29 A

29

Figs. 29 & 29A (opposite page). Rembrandt van Rijn (1606-1669). *The stone bridge*. Rijksmuseum, Amsterdam. Rembrandt also adopted the format used by the majority of Dutch landscape painters, with one third landscape to two thirds dark, stormy sky; but Rembrandt introduced his own use of light, using a strong ray of light to strike the trees near the bridge and leaving the remainder in shaded chiaroscuro, a practice he used with his portrait paintings.

Figs. 30 & 31. Meindert Hobbema. *Marshy woodland*. 1660, Museo Thyssen Bornemisza, Madrid. Hobbema was inspired to paint this picture by an etching made by his master Jacob van Ruysdael, with whom he often used to go out painting from nature. *The avenue at Middelharnis*, National Gallery, London (fig. 31), is the most well known of his landscapes, famous because of its highly original structure. The usual two thirds of sky formula is used, but in this case the sky is punctuated with a double line of trees which reach into the distance. This work had considerable impact on the English landscape artists of the eighteenth and nineteenth centuries.

Fig. 32 (below). Albert Cuyp. *The mass in Dordrecht*, National Gallery, London. His work is similar in format to the works of artists mentioned earlier: his landscapes looked at country themes, he usually included animals in his landscapes and bathed the scenes with warm golden sunlight.

31

32

Italian Landscapes in Oils: Poussin, Claude, Canaletto

Two of the most significant landscape painters in seventeenth century Italy were Frenchmen: Nicholas Poussin (1594-1665) and Claude Lorraine (1600-1682). In 1624, Poussin moved to Rome and, apart from two years spent in Paris, stayed there until his death. Claude, when he was a twelve year old orphan was already in Italy where he spent his entire life apart from a couple of years in Nancy.

Nicolas Poussin is the forefather of French Classical painting, his earlier works were figure paintings and religious themes, he then progressed to mythological scenes, he always surrounded his figures with extensive stretches of impressive landscape. Poussin also painted a number of works where landscape was the main theme of the painting, however, he always included little figures from a mythological story in the foreground (fig. 33).

Claude Lorraine (Claude Gellée, as he is known in France or Claudio de Lorena, el Lorenés in Spain), is one of the most important landscape painters of the eighteenth century. He became orphaned at a very early age and a relative took him to Rome where he became the servant of a landscape painter by the name of Tassi. Five years later he was already assisting Tassi with his paintings. It is known that he knew Poussin and that over a number of years they went drawing and sketching from nature together along with an Italian called Bamboccio and a German, Von Sandrart. Apart from these sketches Claude painted his landscapes in the studio using a formula that generally included a large tree to one side or in the center, balanced by another tree to one side and a building or bridge in the center or to one side. The scenes were backlit and there were figures in the foreground. You can see this typical composition in figure 34, next to a scene of a seaport set in ancient times, a subject that Claude particularly like to paint (fig. 35). Note here the use of backlighting once again.

Giovanni Antonio Canale, known as Canaletto (1697-1768), a native of Venice, was one of the earliest and most influential of the Italian Vedutisti, i.e. painters of topographical, descriptive views of landscape, buildings etc. He was highly skilled at drawing and an exceptional painter. He is most famous for his paintings of Venice, characterised by their luminosity and their strong contrasts of light and shade (fig. 36). Canaletto sketched for some of his paintings from nature, with the use of a camera obscura. He then painted the vedute in the studio, he would develop a solid geometric perspective structure which was then overlaid with details in the studio. Admire the mood of the sky, the green water, the play of light on the buildings and the brightly colored boats and people.

Fig. 33 (below). Nicolas Poussin (1594-1665). *Pastoral scene*. Suida-Manning collection, New York. I'm sure you'll agree that this is a masterpiece, its classicism clearly indicates the identity of the artist. Poussin painted works like this in his studio, but apart from these he made drawings and sketches from nature, usually with watercolor washes with bistre, in the company of Claude.

Figs. 34 & 35 (opposite page). Claude Lorraine. *Idyllic landscape with the flight from Egypt*. Museo Thyssen Bornemisza, Madrid. And *Mist on the sea port*. Musée du Louvre, Paris. Claude Lorraine favored the use of backlighting, using warm tones for the skies and golden twilights. His landscapes were generally on a large scale (*The flight from Egypt* measures 1.93 m high by 1.47 m wide). He painted his works in the studio as Poussin did, taking the drawings and sketches he had made from nature and he combined them to create a composition including their various characteristics.

33

34

35

36

Fig. 36. Giovanni Antonio Canal, Canaletto (1697-1768).*St Mark's Square, Venice*. Museo Thyssen Bornemisza, Madrid. Canaletto started painting as a stage set painter in his father's studio. At twenty two, when he was in Rome, he painted decorations for Scarlatti's Operas and met Panini and Ricci who introduced him to vista painting vedute of cityscapes. This *St Mark's square* is one of his first paintings, dated before 1723, before the square had been paved. It was painted freehand from sketches drawn from nature.

English Watercolor Landscape in the Eighteenth Century

So, what happened to the history of watercolor landscape after Dürer's work in 1495? Absolutely nothing. Watercolor landscape did not put in an appearance for quite some time. In fact, it was neglected as an artistic medium until the middle of the eighteenth century, two hundred and fifty years later. During that period, apart from the occasional watercolor sketch (by Van Dyck for example, fig. 37), watercolor painting, or sepia washes were media for the primary stages of a work, to sketch and experiment on a small scale, for the large figure paintings in oils. They were also used to make studies of landscapes such as those made by Poussin or Claude (fig. 38).

Absolutely nothing that is, until the middle of the eighteenth century, when the English were attempting to open up fields of commerce abroad, coming and going between England and the rest of Europe. This kind of travel became de rigeur, it was the century of the "Great Tour", the century when "The English discovered Rome". When they travelled they would pass through France, Switzerland, Italy and arriving in Rome they would make the obligatory visits to the Coliseum, The Arch of Titus, the thermal baths of Caracalla... and they wanted to take something back to remind them of the Eternal City. What better than a veduta, etchings already existed of the city of Rome. So souvenirs were bought.

Until one day, when the numbers of veduta factories were on the rise in England, somebody had the idea of improving on the black and white prints by overpainting them with watercolors. Paul Sandby was one of the artists involved in this development. He became known by the English as "the father of watercolor". This was because Paul Sandby, instead of running off a production line of identical images ensured that each reproduction had its own unique appearance, an exercise that allowed him to experiment with methods and techniques of working with watercolor (fig. 39). Hence, watercolor landscape painting was developed.

37

38

39

Fig. 37. Anton van Dyck (1599-1641). *Landscape*, watercolor. Institute of Fine Arts Birmingham. Van Dyck painted various watercolor landscapes which he used as studies for oil paintings or as backgrounds to portraits in oils.

Fig. 38. Nicolas Poussin. *The Molle Bridge*. National School of Fine Arts, Paris.

Fig. 39. Paul Sandby. *A path through woodland near Windsor*. Victoria & Albert Museum, London. Paul Sandby perfected his watercolor technique and skills by coloring the etchings printed in black and white and painting the woodland around Windsor. He became an expert and influenced an entire school of English watercolor painting.

English Landscapes in Oils. Gainsborough and Constable

Along with Turner, (who we'll discuss on the following page), Gainsborough and Constable are the three greatest painters of landscape in oils that England produced during the eighteenth and nineteenth centuries.

Thomas Gainsborough (1727-1788) was born in Sudbury, Suffolk. When he was thirteen years old he went to London, where he was apprenticed to Gravelot for a number of years. It appears that he was copying and restoring Dutch paintings by Ruysdael and Hobbema, works that had a considerable influence on his first landscapes. This is clearly evident in his well known work Cornard's Wood (fig. 40), a painting that, according to Gainsborough's own words "I started it before leaving my studies and it was what convinced my father to send me to London".

Landscape painting was Constable's true vocation throughout his life. However, he started to paint portraits from the fifties to earn money, painting full portraits of the whole body, life size, with imaginary landscapes in the background; a format that indicated his rivalry with Sir Joshua Reynolds a painter who was also famous for his portrait paintings and because he was President of the Royal Academy. Despite this fact, it was Gainsborough who the Royal Family commissioned to paint their portraits.

John Constable (1776-1837) started painting in the fields of Suffolk when he was still a schoolboy. "These scenes made me a painter", he claimed. He held his first exhibition in London in 1802 but his work did not initially arouse any great enthusiasm. For a number of years he continued painting, following more or less in Gainsborough's footsteps, until he developed his unique realist style influenced by the success of Ruysdael and the Dutch landscape painters of

the sixteenth century. It was from this period that his paintings show the alterations and contrasts of light and colors, his strong feel for composition and his use of chiaroscuro which he used to unify the painting (figs. 41 & 41A). In 1824 he took part in the Salon de Paris, drawing much admiration from a number of French artists, particularly Delacroix and Bonington. Constable and Delacroix won gold medals for the work they exhibited there.

Fig. 40. Thomas Gainsborough (1727-1788). *Cornard's Wood.* National Gallery, London. This is one of the first pictures painted by Gainsborough. He started it when he was 13 years old and had to leave it unfinished when he went to London, where he had the opportunity to restore and copy paintings by Ruysdael/Ruysdael and Hobbema and finally in 1748 when he was twenty one he returned to alter and finish off the painting.

Fig. 41 (below). John Constable (1776-1837). *The hay wain.* National Gallery, London. In this painting, Constable took his art beyond the influence of the old masters, expressing himself in a more spontaneous and intuitive way. This painting was Constable's first international success, it was exhibited at the Salon de Paris in 1824 and earned much praise from young French artists.

Fig. 41A. *The hay wain* is an example of diagonal composition and dramatic *chiaroscuro*, shaping and molding forms using the contrasts of light and shadow.

40

41 A

41

English Watercolor Landscape: Turner and Girtin

Joseph Mallord William Turner (1775-1851) was an outstanding artist. An exceptional painter of landscapes in watercolor from the age of nine, he colored engravings for a beer dealer from when he was twenty one, when he exhibited his first oil painting in the Royal Academy.

Consider this; at thirteen he was already working as an apprentice to Thomas Malton a watercolorist who taught him the rules of perspective; when he was only fifteen, the Royal Academy accepted one of his watercolors for an exhibition in their galleries; and when he had just turned twenty six he was nominated an Academician of the Royal Academy, something unprecedented at that time. Ever since the death of his father, which left him orphaned, he was a strange character, taciturn and solitary. However, from a young age there was another side to him, valued and admired by contemporary watercolor painters such as Cotman, Varley, Cox, De Wint and particularly Girtin. He became acquainted with them at the house of Doctor Monro, a keen watercolorist who had the idea of starting up an academy for young watercolor painters in his home.

Throughout his life, Turner alternated between using oils and watercolors for his landscapes. It was when he was in Venice for the fourth time that he painted what is considered to be his most breathtaking series of watercolors, remarkable for their treatment light and color, for their technique and simplicity (fig. 42). He also painted the same or similar themes in oils with equal brilliance and mastery.

The French Impressionists commented on his work, "We have been preceded by a great master of the English School, the illustrious Turner".

Fig. 42. J.M.W. Turner. *Venice, San Giorgio Maggiore from the Dogana; Sunset*. Tate Gallery, London. This was painted during his second visit to Venice in 1840. Turner was sixty five years old, an age at which to start taking life at a more leisurely pace.. The watercolor painter William Callow was also staying in Venice at the same time and casually remarked, "One evening when out in a gondola enjoying a cigar, I saw Turner in another gondola painting San Giorgio at dusk. I felt ashamed to find myself indulging in such pleasures while he was working so diligently at such a late hour".

42

43

Thomas Girtin (1775-1802) became a great friend of Turner's when they painted together at Doctor Monro's. Unfortunately he died young, at twenty six and Turner, who imitated his style and felt a great deal of admiration for his friend, commented at his funeral, "If Tom had lived, I would have died of hunger". A slightly exaggerated comment perhaps... In his short life, Girtin excelled through his vision and innovativness with watercolor technique. He used thicker, more absorbent paper than the type that was normally used and he revolutionised the predominant style of the eighteenth century; line drawings highlighted monochrome washes of watercolor, instead he used stronger, more intense watercolors, building stronger contrasts and introducing a more realist style. He set a precedent for the nineteenth century watercolor painters. Look at an example of his style in the picture above, he is still considered a revolutionary of his time (fig. 43).

Fig. 43. Thomas Girtin. *The white house in Chelsea.* **Tate Gallery, London. This is one of the most famous of Thomas Girtin's watercolors because of its restrained palette of two basic colors; burnt Sienna and deep cobalt blue, and because the theme and the composition make it completely distinct from watercolors painted by his contemporaries.**

English Landscapist. Eighteenth and Nineteenth Centuries

What follows now is a brief outline of the key moments in the history of English watercolor landscape during the 18th and 19th centuries. In 1768, the Royal Academy of Arts was founded, its first president was Sir Joshua Reynolds. Amongst the founding members where figures such as the two brothers Paul and Thomas Sandby, both watercolor artists. At the first Annual Exhibition of the Royal Academy, oil paintings were the main feature but there were already a number of watercolorists exhibiting as well. However, watercolor was still not considered a medium comparable to oils and for this very reason there was a clear rule set down for the gallery, watercolor paintings were not admitted unless the artist was also exhibiting oil paintings, oils took up the best positions; they hung in areas that were most visible, occupying the best light, unlike the watercolors. Watercolorists became tired of this humiliating treatment and founded the Society of Watercolor Painters in 1804, which celebrated a year after its foundation with an exhibition exclusively of watercolors (fig. 44). In 1855 Paris hosted the Universal Exhibition, English watercolor painters entered 114 paintings, their quality amazed both the French critics and public. Finally, some thirty years later, in 1881 Queen Victoria decreed that the Society of Watercolor Painters could take the prefix "Royal". By the 19th century, watercolor, and in particular watercolor landscapes were recognised as high art. Apart from Paul Sandby, Turner and Girtin, there were others responsible for this success, namely William Pars, Francis Towne, John Robert Cozens, William Blake, Richard Parkes Bonington, John Sell Cotman, John Varley, Samuel Palmer, David Cox...You will see some examples of the quality of these key figures in the history of watercolor in the following pages (fig. 45, 46 & 47).

44

45

Fig. 44 (opposite page). George Scharf (1788-1860). *The interior of the exhibition gallery of the new Society of Watercolor Painters.* Victoria & Albert Museum, London. Much as it may resemble a color photograph this is actually a watercolor painted in 1808, you can't help but admire the delicacy and fidelity of its execution; the effects of light and shade, the color and the sense of depth and atmosphere implied by the contrast and definition in the foreground in comparison with the light haze in the background.

Fig. 45. Peter de Wint (1784-1849). *The Thames at Windsor.* Collection of the Royal Society of Watercolor Painters, London. De Wint illustrates the use of a sketch technique which focuses on the artistic qualities of the landscape before him, it is a free and fresh approach, with the evident spontaneity of a gifted artist.

46

47

Fig. 47. Richard Parkes Bonington (1801-1828). *The Institute seen from the quayside.* British Museum, London. Born in Nottingham, Bonington went to France as a boy and became a pupil of Gros and he was firm friends with Delacroix who often frequented Gros' studio. *"Watercolorists like Bonington capture such brilliant luminosity in their work that they appear to be like diamonds, bewitching and seducing any spectator who sees them"*, claimed.

Fig. 46. Samuel Prout (1783-1852). *Lucerne.* Collection of the Royal Society of Watercolor Painters, London. Samuel Prout was a contemporary of the great English watercolor painters –Turner, Girtin, De Wint, Blake, Bonington and Cotman. The critic, John Ruskin was one of his most ardent admirers. Prout prompted an interest in picturesque landscape and created a romantic image of England on the continent.

The Impressionists

The first and earliest artist who influenced the Impressionist was Velázquez (1599-1660), whose expressive and supple brushwork and whose loose detail is entirely second to overall the effect which inspired Manet and Monet when they visited the Prado in Madrid; the second was Turner (1775-1851) who, with his *impasto* techniques and *alla prima* approach (faithful to the scene and the moment) was seen as the predecessor of Impressionism; they were also influenced by the nonconformist attitudes of Delacroix (1798-1863) who was a standard bearer for young artists of his time; and the landscapes of Corot (1796-1875), who, from the beginning of his career, was considered a master of Impressionism. Pissarro was a particularly fervent admirer, between 1855 and 1860 he studied with Corot and signed his paintings "Pissarro, Corot's student". Pissarro, recently arrived in Paris, went to Jean-Baptiste Camille Corot's studio and said, "I want to learn to paint like you, Master". Corot answered him:

"**First of all pay attention to drawing and structure; next concentrate on tones and values; after this study the colors; and finally solve how you will implement the painting**".

Corot was a highly skilled draughtsman. His earliest landscapes were based on drawings –exceptionally impressive drawings– executed from nature, in front of the subject, which he would then transform into oil landscapes in his studio. It was only towards the end of his career (from 1865 onwards) that he decided to paint directly from nature (fig. 48), influenced by his "pupils" the Impressionists. Until the

Impressionists, artists would use color ranges which tended towards monochromes of siennas and browns, they would paint with academic fastidiousness, totally lacking in spontinaety. They painted large format works that were slow in their production. Apart from some of the Dutch painters and Constable, Turner and Corot, none of the artists left the studio to compose or paint landscapes. Impressionists painted *á plein air* in the open air, this was one of the regular features of their style. A feature that restricted them to pure colors, and which meant that they had to use a portable easel and medium or small canvases. The time spent on the work was brief, determined by the direction and quality of the light.

The group of "irate young revolutionaries" –as the writer Zola called them–, was originally made up of Manet, Monet, Pissarro, Renoir, Dégas, Cézanne, Boudin, Sisley, Guillaumin, Berthe Morisot, Whistler (who was English) and other lesser known fi-gures (figs. 49, 50 & 51).

Fig. 48 (below). Jean-Baptiste Camille Corot (1796-1875) *The mill at Saint-Nicolas-Les-Arras*. Musée du Louvre, Paris. Corot, who always gave his moral support to the young Impressionists, was himself considered "the great poet of Impressionism" in 1875. This is one of the first landscapes that he painted from nature, breaking with the tradition of developing a landscape in the studio apart from the initial sketches.

Figs. 49 & 49A (opposite page). Alfred Sisley (1839-1890). *The bridge at Hampton Court*. Wallraf-Richartz Museum, Cologne. Along with Monet, Sisley was one of the most quintessential of Impressionists, dedicated almost exclusively to landscape painting. In the schematic diagram (fig. 49A), we can see how Sisley built up a strong composition giving the work a certain unity while the rich range of colors provides an element of variety.

48

Fig. 50. Paul Cézanne. *Mountain Sainte-Victoire*. Metropolitan Museum of Art, New York. In 1902 Cézanne had a studio built on a hillside overlooking Mountain Sainte-Victoire and the city of Aix. From this time, Cézanne painted extensive versions of Mountain Sainte-Victoire –fifty five images in all– a productive exercise and one that evolutionized his painting style.

Fig. 51. Claude Monet. *The station of Saint Lazare*. Fogg Art Museum, Cambridge. In 1877 Monet began a series of paintings on Saint Lazare train station in Paris. He rented a property close to the station and requested permission to paint inside the station, but the crowds would build up around him as he painted and he had to finish his paintings in the studio.

The Post-Impressionists

Paul Gauguin (1848-1903) was one of the artists that exhibited paintings and sculpture in the last four Impressionist Exhibitions (1880, 1881, 1882 and 1886). But after the eighth and final exhibition he left Impressionism behind and painted with ever increasingly bright colors (fig. 52). It was Gauguin who defined Impressionism as *"an artificial form of art, trifling and devoid of intellect"*.

Paul Cézanne (1839-1906), only took part in the first and third of the eight Impressionist exhibitions. It is evident that by 1880 Cézanne had developed a style that distanced him from the Impressionists (fig. 54), he comment-ed that he wanted "to transform Impressionism into something tangible and durable, like the art that is housed in museums". Among the artists who turned away from Impressionism and towards color and creative expression was Van Gogh (fig. 53), an extraordinary artist who constantly made color and dramatic expression a central theme of his work.

So, these were the Post-Impressionists. The name was coined by Roger Fry, an English art critic who, in 1910 organized an exhibition in London which was called Manet and the Post-Impressionists, exhibiting work by Gauguin, Cézanne, Van Gogh, Henri Matisse and Pablo Picasso. *"These artists do more than imitate forms and colors; these artists create forms and colors"*.

Fig. 52 (left). Paul Gauguin (1848-1903). *Tahitian landscape.* **Musée du Louvre, Paris. Gauguin painted this watercolor on his return from Tahiti where he had rejected Western society. Describing this landscape, Gauguin wrote "I wanted to evoke the rich chaos of nature, a tropical sun which burned everything in its path". This same landscape served as a background for one of his last works,** *Women and a white horse.*

52

54

53

Fig. 53. Vincent van Gogh (1853-1906). *King's Canal.* **Private collection. Van Gogh drew this same theme earlier but in daylight, from a normal viewpoint. Here, as a contrast, he painted the canal at dusk and in a very short time, just three hours. He chose an elevated viewpoint, as if he was looking over the canal from a promontory or a bridge.**

Fig. 54. Paul Cézanne (1839-1906). *Landscape in Provence.* **Kunsthaus, Zurich. Cézanne used to go out to paint "with nothing but my little kit of watercolors" as he put it. He liked watercolor because it allowed him to work from nature and quickly, capturing the scene** *au premier coup (alla prima).*

The Fauves

It all happened in the year 1905. Louis Vauxcelles, the critic of an avant garde French art magazine, Gil Blas, went to see the Salon d'Automne. Monsieur Vauxcelles had already heard that this exhibition had caused a stir because of its bright colors. He hadn't anticipated the spectacle that he saw, a riot of strident, impassioned color, violent and wild. Suddenly, M. Vauxcelles noticed a pair of statues in one of the corners of the room, their style was reminiscent of Renaissance sculpture. M. Vauxcelles couldn't contain himself any longer and shouted out *"Mon Dieu! Donatello chez les fauves!"* (My God! Donatello among the wild beasts!)

The phrase and the name fauves stuck, from that moment this style of painting was known as Fauve. Henri Matisse (1869-1954) was the organizer of the Salon d'Automne, this famous exhibition which brought together the Fauvists Derain, Vlaminck, Rouault, Manguin, Camoin, Puy, Friesz and Marquet. It was Marquet who was the creator of the sculptures in a classical style that reminded M. Vauxcelles of the Renaissance artist Donatello.

It was Othon Friesz (mentioned above) who defined fauvist landscape as *"Capturing the sun's brilliance, the technique is based on combining colors with the passion and emotion aroused by nature"*.

As you can see in the images below (figs. 55, 56 & 57), fauvism was a decorative art that played with the vividness and the contrast of colors, however, it was not seen in a good light by the critics or the public at the beginnings of the century. The critic Mauclair defined these paintings as *"paintboxes thrown in the faces of the public"*.

55

56

57

Fig. 55. Georges Braque (1882-1963). *Landscape at L'Estaque.* **Musée de L'Anonciade, Saint Tropez.** In 1906, Braque became part of the group of painters known as the Fauves and exhibited his paintings with them. However, in 1909 he started to work with Picasso and together they created cubism. Picasso and Braque became close friends until 1917 when Braque developed synthetic cubism which distanced him from Picasso.

Fig. 56 (above, right). Raoul Dufy (1877-1953). *Advertising hoardings in Trouville.* **Musée d'Art Moderne, Paris.** Until 1905 Dufy's work would have been described as Impressionist, but that year he was influenced by Matisse's work; the subject matter, compositions. He also became a fauve.

Fig. 57. Maurice Vlaminck (1876-1958). *Rue de Marli-le-Roi.* **Musée d'Art Moderne, Paris.** Vlaminck was a great friend of Derain and shared a studio with him. He was a versatile character; he wrote, played the violin, was a lover of speed and took part in bicycle racing. He was an admirer of Van Gogh, Cézanne and African sculpture.

Cubism, Expressionism and Abstract Art

After the Fauves and the Post-Impressionists came the Cubists, who painted landscapes in which the colors and forms owed much to a style initiated by Cézanne and developed further by Braque and Picasso. There were other artists in addition who had influence on this development such as Juan Gris (1887-1927), and Piet Mondrian (1872-1944) (fig. 60). This period came to an end with Abstract art which was started by Wassily Kandinsky (1866-1944) in 1910. As a prelude to pure Abstract art, Kandinsky painted a number of landscapes such as the one seen in figure 61.

Fig. 58. Oskar Kokoschka. *Dresden Neustadt II.* **Detroit Institute of Arts.**

Fig. 59. Egon Schiele. *Scene of Kruman.* **Gurlitt Museum, Wolfgang.**

Fig. 60. Piet Mondrian (1872-1944). *Eucalyptus.* **Beyeler Collection, Basil.**

Fig. 61 (below). Wassily Kandinsky (1866-1944). *Autumn II.* **The Philips Collection, Washington. Study Kokoschka and Schilele's Expressionist landscapes and note the distorted appearance of the forms. However, they are figurative and represent fields and houses. The forms and colors are no longer figurative in the Cubist and Abstract works of Mondrian and Kandinsky. Landscape art evolutionized into an avant garde art form becoming ever more distant from reality.**

58

60

59

61

Picasso's Landscapes

In a recent exhibition of Picasso's work held in Barcelona called "Picasso, Landscapes, 1890-1912" the sponsor "La Caixa" Bank succeeded in gathering a total of 218 works, among them were drawings and paintings, including 112 landscapes painted in oils by Picasso between the ages of 9 and 31 years old. This exceptional exhibition illustrates Picasso's mastery of painting; at 17 years old, like an impressionist (fig. 62), ten years later, at 27, he had developed into a radical, beyond definition (fig. 63, 64 & 65), painting landscapes, a subject which was not his main line of enquiry.

Figs. 62 to 65. Pablo Picasso (1881-1973).

Fig. 62. *The farmhouse in Quiquet*. Museo Picasso, Barcelona.

Fig. 63. *Landscape. La rue-des-Bois*. Private collection.

Fig. 64. *Houses on a hill. Horta*. Museum of Modern Art, New York.

Fig. 65. *The Harbour at Cadaqués*. Narodni Gallery, Prague.

Here is a list of the dates that Picasso painted these landscapes. Fig. 62, in 1898 when he was 17 years old; fig. 63, in 1908, when he was 27; fig. 64, in 1909, when he was 28 and fig. 65 in 1910 when he was 28. The evolution is extraordinary, from impressionist to cubist-abstract, Picasso is a unique artist.

Contemporary Landscape in Oils and Watercolor

Contemporary landscape painting has not altered radically since the developments at the beginning of this century. The various contemporary paintings –oils and watercolor– which are reproduced here (fig. 66-73), support this argument and you will observe that these landscapes are not painted very differently from those of the Impressionists. I share the opinion of Francesco Calvo Serraller, who was the director of the Prado in Madrid when he commented on contemporary art: *"What we are seeing now in Art is not a creative era, nor is it a scholastic one, what we are seeing is an approach that repeats, albeit with variations, the fundamental beginnings taking place between 1900 and 1920".*

66

67

68

Fig. 66. José Martínez Lozano. *Sea port*, Oil. Private collection.

Fig. 67. Joaquim Mir. *Landscape Vilano-va*, oil. Museum of Modern Art, Barcelona.

Fig. 68. José M. Parramón. *Scene of the Catalan Pyrenees*, oil. Private collection. Barcelona.

69

70

71

72

Fig. 69. Tomás Sayol. *Landscape*. Watercolor. Private collection. Barcelona.

Fig. 70. Vicenç Ballestar. *Snow in Gurb*. Watercolor. Private collection. Barcelona.

Fig. 71. Guillem Fresquet. *The inlet in, Bilbao*. Private collection. Barcelona

Fig.72. Manel Plana. *The pines*. Watercolor. Private collection. Barcelona.

Fig. 73. José M. Parramón. *Landscape in Vigo*. Watercolor. Private collection. Barcelona.

73

Fig. 74. José M. Parramón (b. 1919). *The patio* (detail). Private collection. I painted this picture in oils with hog brushes heavily loaded with paint. I then used a palette knife to give it the smooth surface which removed the *impasto* effect and the traces of brushstrokes.

MATERIALS,
TOOLS
AND TECHNIQUES

The same materials and tools as ever; paints, supports, paintbrushes, palettes, easels... If you are a keen student but have little experience the information and illustrations in this chapter will be very useful to you. If you are an experienced painter in either oils or watercolor, these pages will also be of help, so that you can compare the color ranges and the paintbrushes (how many and what size) that you use in comparison with what I have to suggest. You may also come across a material or tool that is new to you, or that you know little about; paintbrushes made of sable and synthetic mix for example or primer for oil canvases, etc. And as for the techniques. The same goes for them, this may or may not be crucial advice, but it is always good to be reminded of the rules and how to apply them.

Watercolors; Colors, Paintboxes and Palettes

Watercolors are made up of colored pigments of animal, vegetable or mineral origin, which are mixed and bound with water and gum Arabic, glycerine, honey and a preservative. They are divided into the following categories:

Pans of moist watercolor
Tubes of creamy watercolor

There are also pans of dry watercolor, which are low quality products, cheap to buy and suitable for use in schools. Bottles of liquid watercolor are also available, these are used by professional illustrators or in airbrushes.

The pans of moist watercolor are of professional quality. They are available in square or rectangular pans of plastic and in metal paintboxes made of white enamelled steel which contain 6, 12 or 24 colors, you can also buy single pans (fig. 76).

The creamy watercolors are available in tin tubes and they are also of professional quality; they dilute just as quickly in water producing equally transparent colors. The tubes are also available in paintboxes containing 6 or 12 tubes, which can also be bought separately (fig. 77).

As you can see in the illustrations, the paintboxes are designed with compartments built into the double lid made of enamelled steel. These are for testing and mixing colors and one that serves to separate the tubes or pans of color and create a third palette tray. Another useful feature of these paintboxes is that they have a metal ring on the back (right underneath point A) for gripping the box with your thumb.

There are, however, those who prefer to work with a proper artist's palette, particularly those who use the rich

Fig. 75. Miniature watercolour box, especially for making sketches when travelling. When folded it only measures 12.7 x 5.7 x 3.3 cm.

Figs. 76 & 77. Paint boxes with a selection of colours in pans (76) and in tubes of rich liquid (77).

Figs. 78 & 79 (opposite page, above). Palette for painting with pans of moist watercolor.

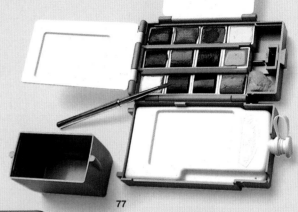

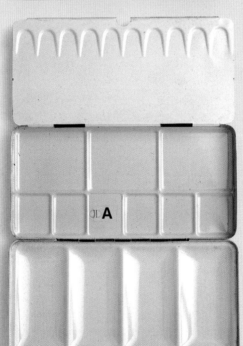

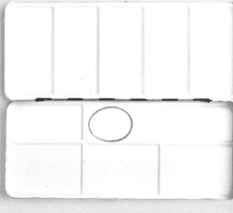

liquid tube paints. Have a look now at figures 78 and 79 which has a ring under the box, also see figure 80 specially for painting with pans of moist color. Which is the best palette? If you paint with tube colors you are definitely better off with the palette in figures 78 or 79. You would find a palette like figure 80 or a paintbox like figure 76 equally convenient when working with moist pans. As for which type of colors are best, the pans or the tubes, it depends entirely on your own preferences. Personally, I have painted with both, it makes no difference to me, I couldn't say that one is better than the other. Basically, when the tube watercolor dries the color is identical to that produced by the watercolor pans.

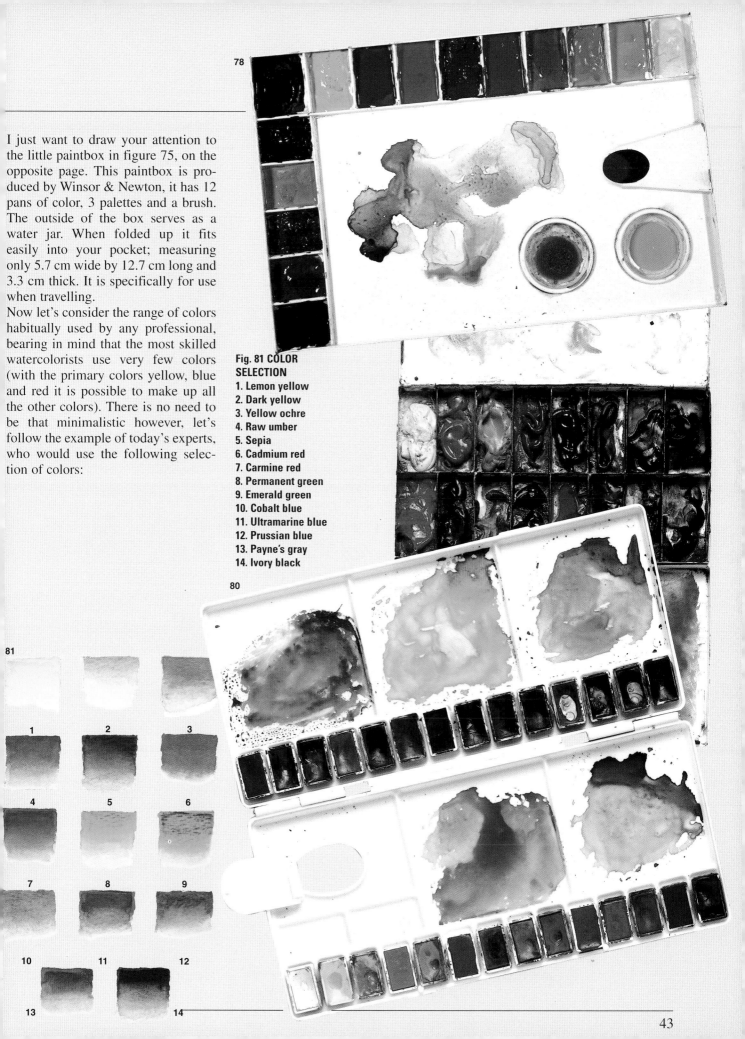

I just want to draw your attention to the little paintbox in figure 75, on the opposite page. This paintbox is produced by Winsor & Newton, it has 12 pans of color, 3 palettes and a brush. The outside of the box serves as a water jar. When folded up it fits easily into your pocket; measuring only 5.7 cm wide by 12.7 cm long and 3.3 cm thick. It is specifically for use when travelling.

Now let's consider the range of colors habitually used by any professional, bearing in mind that the most skilled watercolorists use very few colors (with the primary colors yellow, blue and red it is possible to make up all the other colors). There is no need to be that minimalistic however, let's follow the example of today's experts, who would use the following selection of colors:

Fig. 81 COLOR SELECTION
1. Lemon yellow
2. Dark yellow
3. Yellow ochre
4. Raw umber
5. Sepia
6. Cadmium red
7. Carmine red
8. Permanent green
9. Emerald green
10. Cobalt blue
11. Ultramarine blue
12. Prussian blue
13. Payne's gray
14. Ivory black

Table Easels and Watercolor Paper

The easel in figure 82 is specifically for painting watercolors. Its size allows it to be placed on a table so that the artist can paint sitting down.

The basic characteristics of watercolor paper, apart from its quality, are its thickness and its grain or roughness. Quality is an essential factor; the best producers include their name on one side of the paper, either in print or as a traditional watermark (figs. 83A & 83B).

Thickness is also an important factor. Thin paper does not stand up to the effects of the wet watercolors and will wrinkle or distort; the paper has to be thick, about 300 g per square meter. Ultimately the grain of the paper has an influence on the technique and style of the watercolor, you can chose between A: fine grain paper, B: medium grain or semi-textured paper or C: thick grain paper. The Fine grain paper calls for a far more controlled approach, shading and wet outlines, it speeds up the drying process and accentuates the luminosity of the colors. Medium grain paper allows the artist to work under more controlled conditions, it is highly recommendable for inexperienced students. Thick grain paper is the professional's choice giving greater control of the medium in general (figs. 84, 85 & 86).

Watercolor paper is produced in standard sizes, in blocks mounted on cardboard and in blocks of 20 or 25 sheets which are glued along all four margins, forming a compact brick. This keeps the paper tense as it is being painted on, preventing distortion (fig. 84). Each country tends to have its own sizes. For instance, there are 6 sizes of paper in the UK, the smallest being the Half Imperial, 381 mm x 559 mm and the largest, Antique, is 787 mm x 1346 mm.

82

Fig. 82. Table easel, specially for watercolor painting.

Fig. 83. Watermarks are a characteristic of good quality paper.

Fig. 84. Watercolor paper comes in blocks of 20 or 25 sheets which are glued along all four margins which keeps the paper stretched.

Figs. 85, 86 & 87. The same watercolor painting on fine grain paper, on medium grain and on thick grain (A, B & C).

83 A

83 B

84

85
A

86
B

87
C

Brushes, Water and Implements

There are basically four different kinds of brush for watercolor.

Sable brushes
Synthetic brushes
Mongoose (fitch) brushes
Ox hair brushes

The best of these are the sable brushes, made of Kolinsky sable from the tail of a small breed of mink-like rodent. It is a good brush; absorbent, to "carry" plenty of watercolor, it is flexible, it can splay out like a fan and return to its initial shape and it gives a sharp point. However, they are expensive. Brushes made of synthetic fibres are also good and far more economical. Some factories now produce a brush made up of a combination of sable and synthetic fibre, these are very effective. Although the mongoose brush is somewhat harder than the sable, it is equally compact and also has a good point to it. The ox hair brush is softer and is a popular brush material for the larger sized brushes. Brushes come in different sizes and are graded using numbers, the finest are 0, 1 or 2, up to 14 for sable, and 24 for ox. You should also consider the shape, a flat brush is used as much or maybe more than a round one. I recommend the following selection for watercolor painting; three sable brushes in number 5, 8 and 12, a synthetic brush number 8 and two flat brushes number 14 and 18 made of sable and synthetic fiber (fig. 88).

It goes without saying that water is vital. In the studio you can use a liter jar made of glass with a wide mouth. When outdoors, a plastic jar is easier to prevent breakages (fig. 89).

Finally, have a look at the selection of implements that will come in useful for watercolor painting (fig. 90).

89

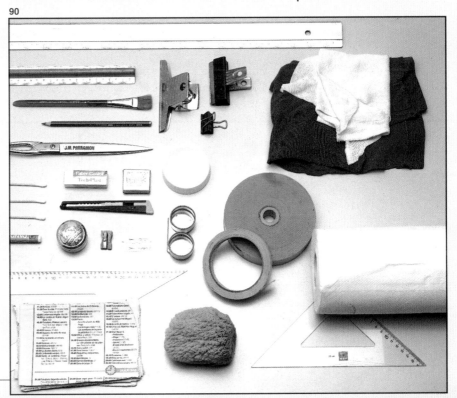

90

Fig. 88 (above). A selection of paintbrushes for watercolor painting: three rounded sable brushes numbers 5, 8 and 12, one synthetic brush, number 8 and two flat brushes made of sable and synthetic fiber, number 14 and 18.

Fig. 89. Water jars, glass for using in the studio and plastic for open air.

Fig. 90. Various implements and materials that are regularly used by watercolor painters.

Materials for Oil Painting

On the left you will see two of the most commonly used easels for oil painting in the studio: the classic tripod which is used in schools and academies and the professional's easel (fig. 91).

The support is generally made of canvas, linen or cotton, mounted on a stretcher or wooden frame. To paint sketches, studies or small scale pictures you can also use cardboard, wood, or canvas covered card which are available in classified sizes in accordance with the International Table of Supports which states the measurements and the proportions of the support dependant on whether it is for portraiture, landscape or seascape (figs. 93 & 94). You could, for example, ask for "a number 15 landscape support". Of course the artist is free to stick to these measurements or order a size proportioned to their needs. Canvas can be bought by the meter as well, in widths of 70 cm or 1.5 m.

The canvases, boards and card for oil paint can be obtained with a primer or a base of glue and *gesso*. These preparations can also be bought in tubes or bottles. Supports of cardboard or paper can also be primed rubbing the surface with a piece of garlic.

Finally, have a look at figure 95; two canvases mounted on frames with pieces of wood stuck in the corner angles to keep the canvas stretched. The metal devices help to transport recently painted canvases so as to prevent smudging.

Fig. 91. Studio easels for painting in oils or watercolor.

Fig. 92. Supports for oil painting: A, primed canvas; B, cardboard; C, wood; D, canvas; E, paper.

Fig. 93. Proportions of standard size canvases: Figure, Landscape and Seascape.

Fig. 94. The table of international canvas measurements.

Fig. 95. Canvases mounted on a carrier.

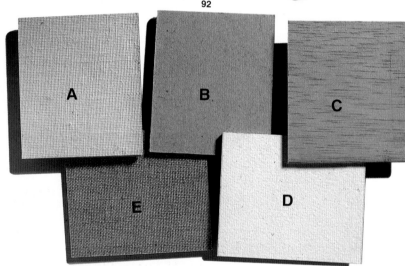

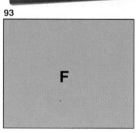

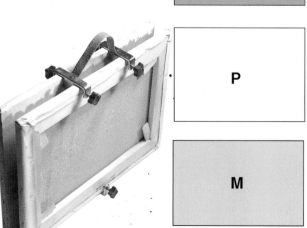

TABLE OF INTERNATIONAL CANVAS MEASUREMENTS

N.°	Figure	Landscape	Marine
1	22 x 16	22 x 14	22 x 12
2	24 x 19	24 x 16	24 x 14
3	27 x 22	27 x 19	27 x 16
4	33 x 24	33 x 22	33 x 19
5	35 x 27	35 x 24	35 x 22
6	41 x 33	41 x 27	41 x 24
8	46 x 38	46 x 33	46 x 27
10	55 x 46	55 x 38	55 x 33
12	61 x 50	61 x 46	61 x 38
15	65 x 54	65 x 50	65 x 46
20	73 x 60	73 x 54	73 x 50
25	81 x 65	81 x 60	81 x 54
30	92 x 73	92 x 65	92 x 60
40	100 x 81	100 x 73	100 x 65
50	116 x 89	116 x 81	116 x 73
60	130 x 97	130 x 89	130 x 81
80	146 x 114	146 x 97	146 x 90
100	162 x 130	162 x 114	162 x 97
120	195 x 130	195 x 114	195 x 97

Oil Paints

Oil paints consist of the same organic pigments as watercolor, however, in this case they are combined and bound with oils, ether based substances, resin, balsams or wax.

Oil paints are sold in tin tubes, the most common size being a number 6 which contains between 20 and 25 ml, except for the color white which is used in greater quantities and comes normally in a number 10, which contains 60 ml (fig. 96). Brands for professionals include names such as Rembrandt de Talens, Winsor & Newton, Schmincke, Lefranc-Burgeois, Grumbacher, Titan, etc. Oil paints are expensive. Some professionals use studio quality paints which are cheaper and of acceptable quality; recommended brands to buy are Delbe, Ticiano, Lefranc-Burgeois-Études, etc. (fig. 97).

I have also made a list of colors here, which can be limited to 12, including white. You can see the color range on the right (fig. 98). You will see in the corresponding list that I have marked some of the colors with an asterisk, you could make do without these colors if necessary.

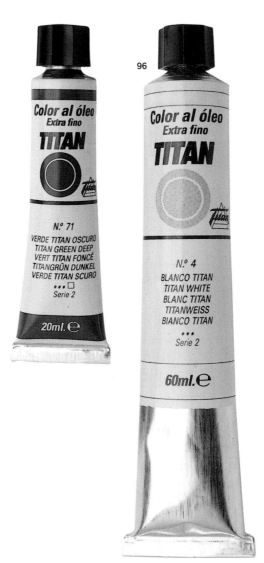

Fig. 98. COLOR SELECTION, OIL PAINTS

1. Titanium white	7. Crimson madder
2. Lemon yellow	8. Burnt umber
3. Dark yellow*	9. Emerald green
4. Yellow ochre	10. Cobalt blue
5. Burnt umber*	11. Ultramarine blue
6. Light vermilion	12. Prussian blue

Fig. 96 (above). Volume of oil paint tubes, number 6, 20 ml and number 10, 60 ml.

Fig. 97. Studio quality oil paints.

Paintbox, Palette and Brushes

Thinners: the most popular is linseed oil, which is thick and slow drying and turpentine (turps), a solution that dries very rapidly, used by many professionals as the only thinner, I use it because of its matt finish. Mixing both thinners in equal amounts results in a good medium or balanced thinner. It is useful to have a paintbox to paint sketches or as a simple workbox (fig. 99). Apart from keeping tubes of color, brushes, palette knives, thinners and your palette, it comes in useful for painting sketches outdoors, thanks to two useful details, on both sides of the lid, it has grooves which enable you to safely carry around recently painted sketches.

Have a look at the palette in figure 100. It is a rectangular one , made of wood, the most popular one both for painting outdoors and in the studio as you will see. Note how the palette is supported by the thumb of the left hand, which supports it and holds the brushes and a cloth at the same time. The right hand works with the brush, mixing colors and applying them to the canvas. The little containers that you can see are for holding linseed oil and turps, the colors are arranged in a specific order, from lightest to darkest; white is followed by the warm color range then by the cool color range. You can copy this or order them as you please, but always use the same sequence so that you can locate the color without thinking about it as you paint.

Finally, it is useful to know that many artists have a palette in their studio that is simply a piece of wood placed on top of a piece of furniture or small table (fig. 101).

Fig. 99. Paintbox for transporting materials, including the palette and a recently painted board supported by wooden strips.

Fig. 100 (below, right). Palette with a selection of oil paints. Colors are in a specific order.

Fig. 101 (below, left). Studio palette consistin of a board on top of a small table.

103

PAINTBRUSH SELECTION

Hog bristle:
Two rounded brushes number 6
Two flat brushes number 8
Two filbert brushes number 10
Two flat brushes number 12
One filbert brush number 12
One filbert brush number 14
One flat brush number 18
One flat brush number 20

Sable or synthetic fiber:
One rounded brush number 4
One rounded brush number 6
One rounded brush number 8

105

Fig. 102. A selection of filbert brushes for oil paints.

Fig. 103 (left). Three types of brush: rounded, flat and filbert.

Fig. 104. A regular selection of brushes for oil painting.

Fig. 105. Palette knife.

Paintbrushes for oils

The paintbrushes commonly used for oil painting are made of hog bristle and like those used for watercolor they are available in different thicknesses, which are labelled from 0 to 24, going up in even numbers (fig. 102). The brush head can be shaped three different ways: rounded, flat or filbert (fig. 103). Painting in oil it is normal to work with four or more brushes at a time so that you can change color and brush size as you paint. Painting in oil you can also use fine sable or synthetic brushes for fine details. It is important that for oil painting you have a wide range of brushes to hand, thirteen or fourteen brushes of hog bristle, sable or synthetic fiber (see the list above, fig. 104).

A palette knife is also vital, it should be trowel shaped like a builder's tool, it can be used to alter the paint applied by scraping recently applied paint and for cleaning the palette (fig. 105). You will also need cloths and pieces of newspaper for wiping paint off the brushes and cleaning them.

Equipment for Painting Outdoors

Fig. 106. Here is a selection of equipment normally used by a professional to paint oils outdoors. It consists of the classic easel; box and frame that folds up to make it easy to carry. All the materials can be carried inside; palette, thinner containers, colors, brushes, palette knife, charcoals, jars and containers with linseed oil and turps, and the canvas of course. Your equipment should also include a folding seat and cloths. You may also wish to take a hat and a radio or walkman.

107

Fig. 107. This is the equipment for watercolor painting outdoors. You need practically the same as you would to paint in oils, that is, a folding easel with storage space and a wooden board onto which the watercolor paper is mounted (this work should be done beforehand in the studio as it involves dampening the paper, applying it stretched to the board using sticky tape to hold it firmly and letting it dry so that it becomes taut) and using the drawer in the easel as a resting place for the watercolor palette or paintbox. A hat, cloths to wipe the brushes, a radio walkman and finally a jar of water.

Oil Painting Techniques

First we are going to discuss the three most common ways of using the paintbrush, then we will consider the principle of painting fat over lean in

108

order to avoid subsequent cracking of the picture surface.

In the images above you can see three distinct ways of holding the brush.

The first (fig.108), is the normal way, i.e. holding it just as you would a pencil or a pen for writing, you simply hold the stem further up. This allows you freedom of movement in any direction; upward, downward, to one side, just by turning the brush. You can see that in this position without bending the brush's fibres you can paint a dot, a line or a delicate stroke

etc. and by varying the amount of pressure that you apply you can paint with wide, firm, energetic strokes.

109

In the second image, *painting with the side of the brush*, the hand has simply turned 45° towards the right, forming an oblique angle with the picture plane, to paint "going over" applying the brush flat, in a less energetic way.

Finally, in figure 110 *with the brush handle in the hand*, this helps you to paint in a looser, more carefree way, synthesizing the work, passing over little details, sometimes applying more paint to an area that has already been painted to bring out a lighter color over a darker one for example.

Fat over lean. The first coats of a painting have to be lean, which means that they should be thinned with turps. If the first coats are applied with oil

110

paint thinned with linseed oil this is a fat solution, and if the successive layers of paint are lean, i.e. dissolved with turps, then the last lean coat will dry faster than the fat coats beneath. When this happens the surface will contort and crack, in time the painting will appear riddled with cracks (fig. 111).

111

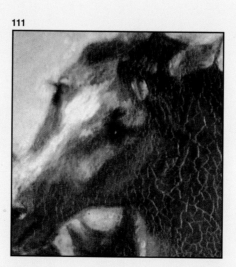

Figs. 108, 109 & 110 (above). Different ways of holding the paintbrush when painting with oils; the regular way and holding the handle inside the hand.

Fig. 111 (left). Eugène Delacroix (1798-1863). *Arab on horseback* (detail). Hermitage Museum, St Petersburg.

Looking After Your Paintbrushes

Paintbrushes are expensive but if they are well cared for they will last for years. They must be carefully washed when the painting is finished, presu-

112

115

117

hes for a couple of days then leave them on a plate with the bristles submerged in water (fig. 112). Just remember that this should not be stan-

113

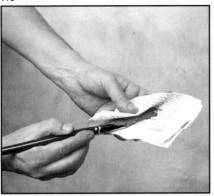

116

118

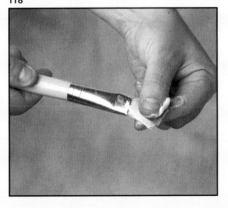

small quantity of turps (fig. 114). With the brush soaked in turps rub the brush onto a cloth, firmly pinching the bristles. Keep doing this a few times

114

until the brush is leaving hardly any traces of color (fig. 115).

Now start the washing process. Wet the brush with water and rub it against a bar of mild soap (fig. 116). Next, rub the brush in the palm of your hand, the soap should produce a froth tinted with color (fig. 117). Immediately, wash away the soap with water and repeat the operation by rubbing it on the soap bar again and rubbing it in the palm of your hand. You can alternate this method with another which is to pinch the crown of bristles squeezing out the soap and paint as you can see in figure 118. Keep repeating this until the soap froth is colorless. Wash out the brush with water once more and dry it with a towel, smoothing out the bristles to reshape them. Now the brush is ready, you've finished.

ming that the artist is not going to continue with another painting straight away or the following day. Follow this advice for the best way to clean your brushes.

First, I want to point out that if you leave an unwashed brush loaded with paint for five or six days the paint will dry and the brush will be ruined. If you need to put off washing the brus-

dard practice.

So let's apply ourselves to the task of washing the brushes one by one. First, take the brush and wipe off excess paint by pinching the bristles of the brush with a piece of newspaper. I would use about an eighth of a page (fig. 113).

Next, submerge the brush –dip it in just briefly!– in a pot containing a

Figs. 112 to 118. Cleaning brushes used for oil painting. This is a complicated and boring job which you can put off for a couple of days by leaving the brushes on a plate, their bristles submerged in water (fig. 112), but sooner or later you will have to carefully go through with the cleaning process.

Oil Painting Techniques

Lluís Pasqual, director of the Odéon Theatre in Paris once spoke of the concept of technique, *"When a great show is discussed there is always talk of technique. More's the pity, it is an indication that the show didn't come up to their expectations. Technique is like glass, when it is flawless you don't comment on it, you can't see it"*. This parallel is applicable when talking of techniques of oil painting and particularly when talking of watercolor. When these techniques are well employed they are not commented on, you don't notice them. Let us look closely at some of the following techniques.

Fig. 119. Heavily thinned paint. A technique applied by artists including Dégas in *The absenthe drinker* (Musée d'Orsay, Paris). The technique consists of painting with very dilute paint, thinned with turps or a mixture of linseed oil or turps.

Fig. 120. Painting with *impasto*. Van Gogh is well known for his *impasto* techniques, have a look at this detail of *The seed sower* (private collection, Switzerland). The impasto is applied using thick oil paint, which requires quite considerable practice.

Fig. 121. Rectifying mistakes with a palette knife. It is perfectly normal to make mistakes, don't worry, they can be removed effectively with a palette knife, which scrapes away the paint and leaves the surface beneath for you to reapply the paint.

Fig. 122. Rubbing out with a cloth. If you cannot remove all the paint using a palette knife you can rub at the canvas with your index finger wrapped in a cloth.

Fig. 123. *Veladura* (veils of color). This consists of applying a transparently fine layer of paint over another layer of previously applied color in order to alter its shade.

Fig. 124. Rubbing in color. When the oil paint has the right consistency, just when it is beginnning to dry, this is the right moment to rub the brush, thickly loaded with color, dark or light, onto the form that is being shaped.

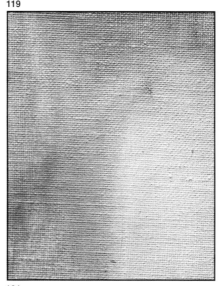
119

120

121

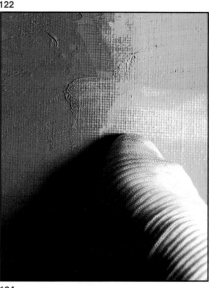
122

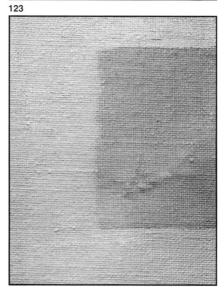
123

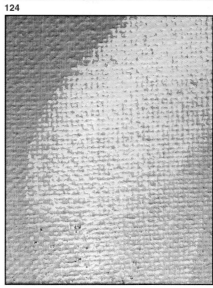
124

125

126

127

128

129

130

Fig. 125. Techniques for painting on wet. In order to add a detail, e.g. the bare branches of a tree, over a recently painted area, you have to use a sable brush, loaded with diluted paint, applying the color very gently.

Fig. 126. Using a mahlstick. A mahlstick is a wooden pole with a wad of material in a ball bound to one end. The artist uses it to support the hand holding the paintbrush, to steady his hand when painting precise details.

Fig. 127. *Sgraffito*. The example here is a detail of Rembrandt's painting *Portrait of the artist's mother* (Von Bohlen und Halbach collection, Essen). The criss-crossed lines at the neck of the dress have been made by scratching with the point of the brush's handle, so the light color was painted over a dry area that is darker and then the new paint is scraped away to reveal color underneath.

Fig. 128. *Pentimento*. This is a detail from a painting by Velázquez, *Felipe IV on horseback* (Prado, Madrid). Can you make out a third leg, just behind the two back legs of the horse, overlapping with the horse's left leg? This was a mistake that was altered by Velazquez which, in time, has reappeared in the painting. This just goes to show how common it is to make alterations to paintings.

Fig. 129. Painting with your fingers. According to Jacobo Palma, who regularly visited Titian's studio, he *"would paint with his thumb and with two extended fingers he would spread the paint and mix it into subtle mixes of color"*.

Fig. 130. Whiter clouds. Consider using your palette knife to apply white paint, e.g. when painting clouds. You simply have to "smooth" the paint on, pressing the white mass and extending it to apply a layer of pure white paint.

Watercolor Painting Techniques

131

132

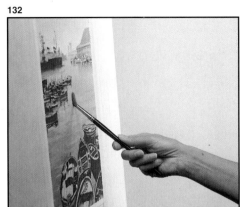

Fig. 135. Wash the brush again, drain it off like before and continue diluting it until you reach the base of the rectangle.

If necessary you can retouch the bottom part, absorbing more or less water with the brush while diluting. For good blending you can incline the board in a horizontal, diagonal, or vertical position as necesary.

Look at the two basic ways of holding the brush, the same as in oil painting. The regular way; as if it were a pencil but holding the handle further up (fig. 131) and with the handle inside the hand (fig. 132).

Let's start with a few basic practical exercises that I suggest you follow, unless of course you already have plenty of experience in which case you can turn over to page 58.

Dry wash

Start by drawing a rectangle approximately 15 x 20 cm with an HB pencil. Fix the paper with a few clips to a board and angle the board on an incline, almost vertical, on a table easel or leaning the board between your lap and the table. Prepare a jar with water and a number 14 sable or synthetic brush. Prepare a color, cobalt blue for example in a small container and...

Fig. 133. ...start with an intense stroke of color, working from right to left a the top of the rectangle.

Fig. 134. Make this quick! Wash the brush, load it with water, gently drain some of the water and apply the brush to the middle of the base of the stroke of color, dissolving it and diluting the color, keep painting from side to side towards the base using horizontal strokes.

133

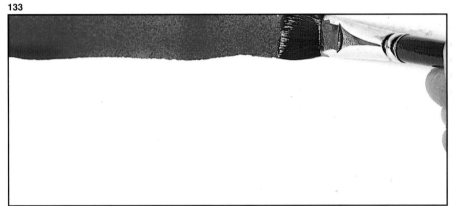

134

135

136 **137** **138**

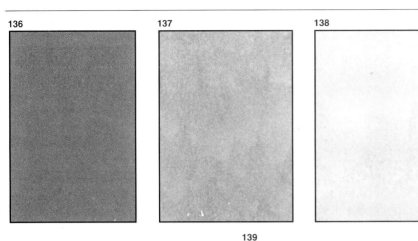

Figs. 136, 137 and 138. Shading in different tones. This exercise consists of painting three rectangles of 15 x 20 cm, with shades of the same color, red carmine, but in different tones. As you already know, the shading must be started with brushstrokes from side to side at the top of the rectangle, then continue painting with horizontal strokes, spreading the color from top to bottom, until you arrive at the base of the rectangle where any excess drops of paint must be soaked up.

Wet Wash

As a rule watercolor is applied on dry, but there are occasions –when painting skies for example– that you may want to paint on wet, i.e. wetting the paper with water and applying the paint onto a damp surface, this is normally called painting wet on wet, something that we are going to practice right now by painting this stormy looking sky.

139

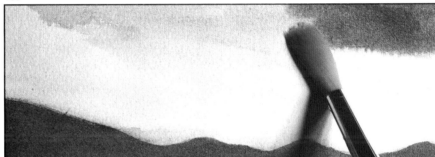

140

141

Figs. 139, 140, & 141. First step. Wet the paper using a wide brush and applying brushstrokes of clean water. Keep the board and the paper inclined at an angle of 60 or 75°. Wait for the water to dry a little and when the paper is no longer wet but still damp apply a thick, horizontal brushstroke of solid color (fig. 139), wait to see if the color runs and absorbs into the wet paper, and add more touches of color (fig. 140), or with delicate touches of the brush start to give shape to the form that you wish to create.

Watercolor Painting Techniques

The techniques employed in watercolor painting are more complicated than those used in oil painting. This is mainly because of the fact that watercolor is transparent rather than opaque and has no covering power. When painting with oils for example, the painter does not have to reserve white spaces, oil is opaque and you can apply white or any pale color on top of a dark color. However, the color white does not exist in watercolor painting, the white is obtained from the white of the paper and there are more than five different methods or techniques you can use in order to reserve or create patches of white. Remember "...technique is like glass, when it is flawless you don't comment on it, you can't see it". These techniques must be used having studied and understood their applications.

Let's have a look at this subject by considering the following illustrations.

Figs. 142 & 143. Lifting off white spaces on wet. When dealing with recently painted watercolor, wash the brush with water and rub it with a cloth. Then apply it to the wash and see how it absorbs the color and opens a white space, so that you could, for example, add a cloud to the sky as the artist here has done.

Figs. 144 & 145. Lifting off white spaces on a dry wash. Put a sizeable drop of water onto area where you want to lift off the white space, applying it with a synthetic brush (somewhat firmer than a sable brush, fig. 144). Wait a couple of minutes until the paint has been dissolved by the water. Wash and dry the brush, then apply it to the area, rubbing gently and absorbing the water, repeat this action until a white space appears. If the resulting area is not totally white you can resort to using a few drops of bleach.

Figs. 146 & 147. Masking white with latex. Apply the latex to the small detail or area that you wish to reserve. Paint the subject in watercolor

and then remove the latex by rubbing at it with your fingers or with an eraser. Then add the finishing touches to the subject. When applying the latex don't use a sable brush, but a synthetic one, which should be washed with soap and water immediately after use.

Fig. 148. Masking with wax. Use white wax to draw in the small areas or shapes

142

144

146

148

you want kept white and paint over with watercolor. The areas sealed with wax remain white as the wax repels the water.

Fig. 149. Latex white spaces with a fingernail. Using the nail of your little finger you can lifting off white spaces on a dark wash that has recently been painted and is still damp. There are also paintbrushes

143

145
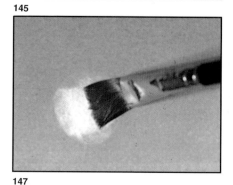

147

149

with shell handles that have a bevelled edge which you can use in the same way, but you can use the end of any brush handle to good effect.

Fig. 150. Lifting off white spaces with sandpaper. When the water-color has dried completely you can use very fine sandpaper to lifting off whi-

te spaces simply by rubbing it fairly briskly onto the area you want to alter.

Fig. 151. Creating textures with water or turpentine. Painting on wet you can achieve certain special effects simply by loading the brush with clean water and applying it to an area that has recently been painted. You can

achieve similar results by applying turps using the same technique.

Fig. 152. Dry brush technique. Consists of painting with a brush loaded with paint but with hardly any water, so that when you apply the brush the rough texture of the paper is highlighted through the brushstrokes as you can see in the picture.

Fig. 153. Testing shades and colors. Leave a blank margin of 3 or 4 cm down the right of the paper to be used as a space for testing colors and shades. Mariano Fortuny put this into practice.

Figs. 154 & 155. Creating textures with salt. If you throw kitchen salt –all the better if the crystals are a little bigger– onto a wet wash of fairly intense color, it will absorb the color and create a curious texture which is evident when the wash has dried and the grains of salt are rubbed off gently with a hand. You can use this effect for backgrounds, walls, mountains, skies, etc.

Figs. 156, 157 & 158. Flicking or spraying. To darken a sky like this or any other background you can shade or vary the area by using a toothbrush loaded with color which you drag over the teeth of a comb. First you should cut out shapes to correspond to the forms you want to shield. You can see the final appearance of this technique in figure 158. A few lines have been added to outline the shapes.

150

151

152

153

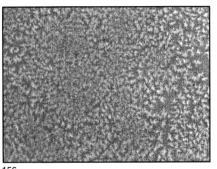

154

155

156

157

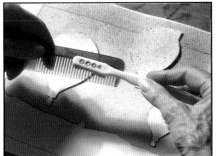

158

Fig. 159. José M. Parramón (b. 1919). *Landscape in Vigo* (detail). Private collection. I chose this subject thinking that the wet on wet watercolor technique, which you can see clearly in the background, would be most suitable. It is also an invitation to apply the theory of near and far colors, in this case by using yellows and greens in the foreground, the greens of the fields, the bluish green of the trees and the blue of the mountains in the background. This is a theory that is discussed further in the following pages.

DRAWING, SELECTING THE SUBJECT

What guidelines or rules did Van Gogh, Monet or
Cézanne use to choose a subject for their paintings? Is it
certain that they simply painted the first thing that came
to hand and that they agreed with the famous quote by
Renoir, "Themes, motifs, I solve that problem with the
first thing that falls my way!". Yes and No. This is
a subject that we are going to study in the following
pages but first some drawing exercises. As Ingres said
—and he was right— "You paint as you draw".
So let's look over the technical rules of dimensions and
proportion, the importance and value of preliminary
sketches and the rules of perspective which are crucial
to any work. We will finish up with a couple of practical
exercises, studying Monet's technique in oils
and Turner's watercolor technique.

Calculating Dimensions and Proportions

The following pages will serve as a practice aid for the calculation of dimensions and proportions. Our subject is a landscape, our task, to make a preliminary sketch for a painting.

How do I start, with a pencil or a paintbrush? The eternal question. There are those who make sketches using paint right from the onset, with a few lines and marks, shading the dark areas, observing the colors accurately. Having said that, the regular and recommended approach for a student is to make an initial sketch with charcoal, a medium that is easy to rub out with a soft eraser or even with a cloth. To finish the sketch, firm up the lines of the drawing and add some shading, fixing the drawing with aerosol fixer when finished. Wait a few minutes to let the fixer dry before starting to paint.

Fig. 160. I am going to carry out the exercise now, starting with a support of number 10 landscape canvas (30 x 58 cm), a charcoal pencil and a soft malleable eraser. First step, I observe, study, focus on the subject constantly as I consider the mental calculations of dimensions and proportions. I start by drawing a horizontal line dividing the canvas in half and bisecting it with a vertical line.

Fig. 161. I continue with the mental calculations, discovering that the closest corner of the church coincides with the vertical guideline, from this vertical I draw a freehand line at an angle which corresponds to the lower edge of the church's roof, and then I finish off the roof lines. Take note that the width of the church from the corner coinciding with the vertical guideline to the bell tower measures a quarter of the length of the right hand section.

Fig. 162. Next I note that the highest point of the bell tower (A) is half the total distance (a'-a') from the central horizontal to the top of the picture. This allows me to draw in the bell tower freehand and the base line of the church and the houses on the right (C).

Fig. 163. Before you continue, just a quick digression: finding the correct distances and proportions relies on keeping subsequent sketching consistent with what you already have on paper and on the tried and tested method of studying the model measuring and dividing it into parts with a pencil or brush held out at arm's length. Let's go on...

160

161

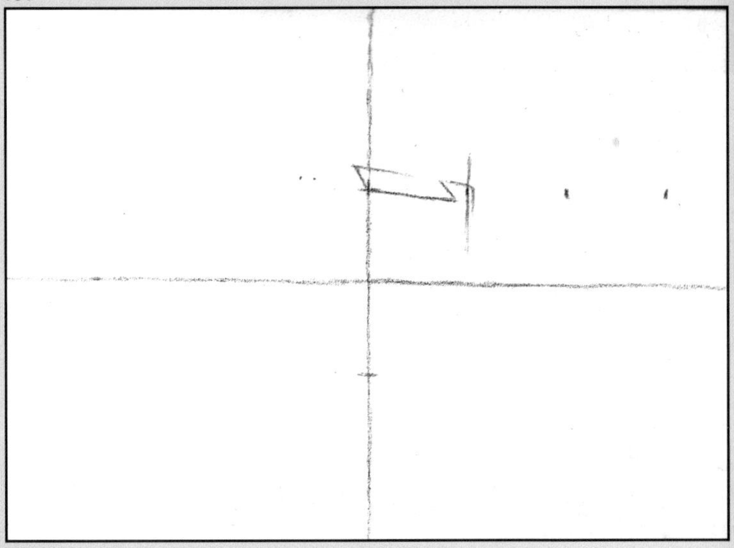

162

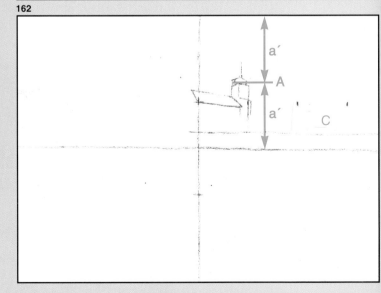

Fig. 164. Comparing dimensions, I see that the point D, the center of the bell tower, and point F, the corner of the church on the left, are equidistant from the vertical line down the center. This distance (b'b') allows me to draw the lines that shape the structure of the church, noting at the same time that the distance (b') between the edge of the church (F) and the limit of the trees (G) is the same as the other measurements.

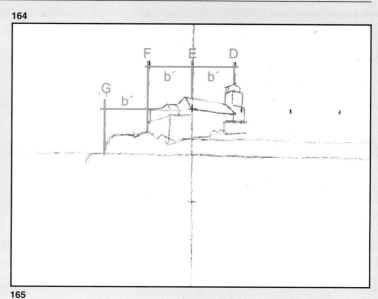

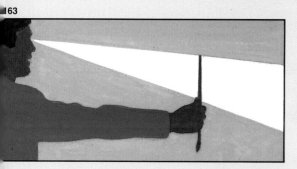

Fig. 165. Now I am going to draw the row of houses on the right hand side. With the aid of a pencil I discover that the left hand edge of the house in the center (H) bisects the distance between the center of the picture and the right margin. Having drawn in the house I add the dimensions of each other house by eye. When the roofs and windows have been added the houses are finished.

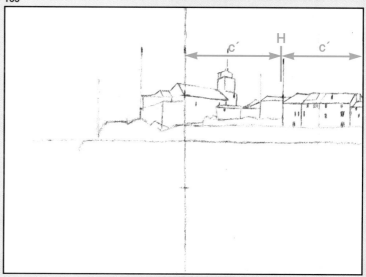

Fig. 166. I continue to develop the image in the same way, simplifying foreground shapes into cubes. How and where should you place that building? Measure and compare the distances with the pencil, you'll find that the horizontal guideline (d' to d') divides the distance in half between the top of the bell tower and the base of the building in the foreground. When the base has been drawn in, compare the width of the bell tower with the width of the foreground building. Once I have determined this width I add the walls and complete the square by adding a line across the top. Then I make it into a cube by adding the lines of recession. I then divide the front face of this cube with a horizontal line that continues to the left, becoming the base line for the group of houses in the bottom left quadrant of the image. Then I add a few sketchy lines and shadows to shape the area surrounding the building in the foreground.

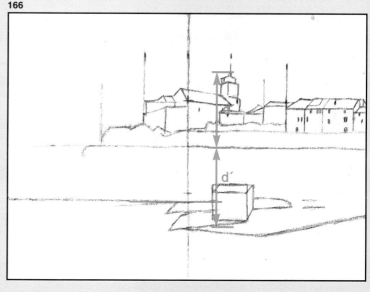

Calculating Dimensions and Proportions

Fig. 167. "Divide and Conquer". Next I start on the group of houses on the left by looking for the central point in the group. I sketch in a line on the right (J) and by extending the horizontal (e' - e') From this line to the extreme left of the drawing, I then find the house in the center of this quadrant (K). First I add this building and using this as a starting point I continue to add those around it, sketching in the roofs and facades by eye. I find that at this stage something that I term a tacit understanding between mind and hand comes into play, in other words the links between mental calculation of the picture's space and dimensions begin to develop almost without conscious effort.

Figs. 168 and 169. Now, at this stage there is hardly any delay in finishing the drawing, then all that is left to do is add the play of light and shadow over the scene and to spray fixer over this study of dimensions and proportions.

Fig. 170. On the subject of fixing a sketch in charcoal on a canvas ready for painting in oils, let me point out that you can also rub the charcoal drawing into the canvas with a cloth, although I recommend that you fix the drawing as you keep a clearer image with more precise lines and details. Bear these two hints in mind: first, fix the drawing with the canvas in a horizontal position, and second, fix it by applying the spray in short bursts, allowing time for the liquid fixing agent to dry. This will prevent an excess of liquid building up and running down the canvas which could smudge or even ruin the sketch.

167

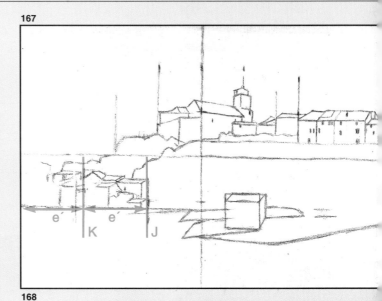

168

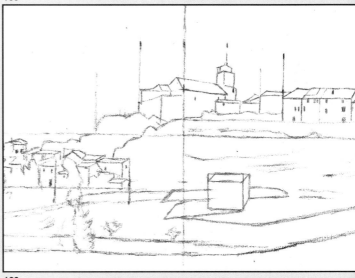

169

170

The Schematic Drawing

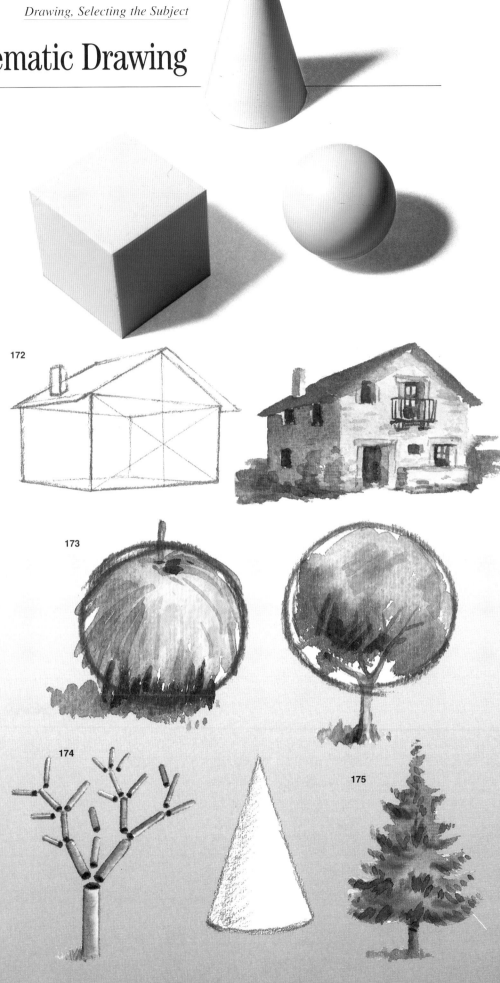

To make a schematic drawing, implies to simplify forms, reducing them to basic boxes, basic forms such as a cube, cylinder, pyramid, sphere, square, rectangle, circle or triangle. This brings to mind a famous quote by the painter Cézanne (fig. 171), when he commented to his colleagues *"Every object can be simplified into the form of a cube, a cylinder or a sphere"*.

So, when faced with an object to draw, the best thing to do is simplify the form. Draw a cube to represent a house or building (fig. 172), a circle or sphere to suggest the shape of a haystack or the crown of a tree (fig. 173), a series of cylinders to construct a tree (fig. 174), a cone to capture the shape of a fir tree (fig. 175), etc. Don't forget that the professional can draw a house, haystack, tree crown, branches, fir tree, etc. without the aid of a schematic drawing.

Also bear in mind that starting your drawing with a schematic drawing of the features, it will be easier to determine the dimensions and proportions of those objects in relation to one-another.

Fig. 171 (above). Paul Cézanne. *Self portrait*. Musée d'Orsay. Paris.

Fig. 172 to 175. A cube, a sphere, a series of cylinders, a cone, etc. These are geometrical forms that can be used to draw a house, a haystack or a tree.

The Preparatory Study

Whether painting in oils or watercolors, all professional painters will carry out a preparatory study. As Maurice Denis said to one of his pupils, *"Before painting a picture, make a rapid sketch and do not even consider deviating from this <u>first, fresh impression</u> for anything in the world"*.

I have underlined "first, fresh impression" because the drawing or study is an attempt –a drawing or painting– in response to your first impression, when you interpret the subject from what you see and what captures your imagination from the start. *"I'll paint the sky bluer, those trees will be darker, this field is going to be lighter..."* i.e. before the factual reality of the model starts to dominate what your imagination sees. To this end, Claude Monet the famous Impressionist painter exclaimed, *"I am wasting too much time being influenced by the model I see in front of me!"*, an aspect that we will discuss further when studying how to interpret landscape.

And my recommendation is never to abandon *the fresh impression*. It is the same as painting a picture thinking of it as if it were a sketch as I have done in my own sketch books. "A creative philosophy springing from unforeseen adventure, from spontaneity and from absolute freedom of expression, complete disregard for the fact that you are drawing or painting a study and not the definitive painting". You will see how a study progresses step by step in the following pages.

Fig. 176. This is the subject, with a tree and a well in the foreground and a house in the background.

Fig. 177. The drawing starts with a horizontal and a vertical guideline which is traced to form a cross in the center in order to help calculate dimensions and proportions. See how the foundation of the house coincides with the horizontal guideline while the wall of the house on the left lines up with the vertical guideline.

Fig. 178. I paint the sky with a series of dispersed cumulus clouds and add the tree in the foreground in a dark –almost black– color, leaving the trunk and a few branches unpainted. I sketch in the tree in the background, behind the house.

Fig. 179. I start to describe the house and the outhouse, altering the gray colors I see to a whitewash with bluish shadows made up of Prussian blue, a little burnt umber and a touch of carmine mixed with white. I paint the trees in the background, the earthy colors of the more distant fields

–yellow ochre, a touch of carmine, and an even tinier bit of cobalt blue to make it a little grayer, a little more carmine in the redder patches– and I start to paint the green fields with emerald green, ochre and white.

176

177

178

179

Fig. 180. I alter the sky. The scattered clouds were too eye-catching, too much of a threat to the unity of the picture. I think it's better now, don't you? I have also practically finished the foreground and the track that gives perspective to the painting.

Fig. 181. The finished study. I have added further detail to the tree in the foreground, the well and the trees behind it, the field with flowers, and I've added the windows and doors to the house and the outhouse. Look carefully at the diversity of tones and colors in the darkest areas of the trees in the foreground and behind the well. This enriches the *chiaroscuro* without understating the contrasts.

180

181

Basic Perspective

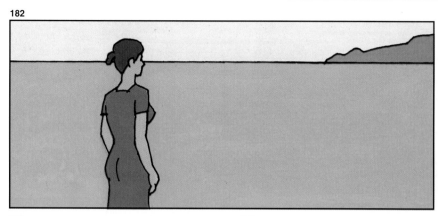

182

But is perspective really necessary for painting landscape? Just read what Van Gogh wrote in a letter to his brother on the subject:

"In London I often stopped to draw along the quays of the Thames when I was walking home from Southampton Street in the evenings, and it was a waste of time. If only someone had talked to me about what perspective was...! How much trouble I could have saved myself! How much more would I have progressed!"

Well, we are not going to discuss all of the pitfalls of perspective, and there are many of them –I've written two books on that very subject– we are simply going to look at the basic rules of perspective that you need for landscape painting. Enough to draw a house, a row of buildings, clumps of trees, a road or a path, etc. You may well know some of the facts that I am going to discuss, in which case you can skip these pages or just read them over to jog your memory about the fundamental rules of perspective. First consider these:

– The horizon line HL
– The vanishing points VP

the horizon line is an imaginary line which is always found in front of us at eye level, when looking ahead, as happens when you are looking at the sea (fig. 182). If you raise your position the horizon line rises with you (fig. 183) and if you lower your position the horizon line sinks too (fig. 184).

The vanishing points are situated on the horizon, they are the points where the lines perpendicular to the horizon coincide. From this you can deduce that there are two basic forms of perspective:

Parallel perspective with one vanishing point (fig. 185).
Oblique perspective with two vanishing points (fig. 186).

(There is another form, aerial perspective which has three vanishing points but I am not going to discuss it as it is not used in landscape painting).

In cases such as the watercolor on the follow-ing page, in which the artist makes a study of a Venetian door (figs.

183

184

185

Fig. 185. Parallel perspective, with one vanishing point.

186

Fig. 186. Oblique perspective, with two vanishing points.

187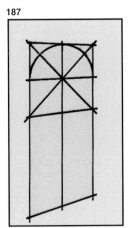

187 A

188

187 & 187A), it is interesting to remember the simple formula to divide a space in perspective to determine its center. A formula that is well known by the professional artist who would no doubt be able to resolve it by eye.

Before a subject like this (fig. 188), in order to determine the distance which separates the different elements, whether they be trees, fence posts, columns of a building or cloister, etc. Study the formula set out below (figs 189-192). Bear in mind that, once again, the professional can solve these issues by eye, simply calculating the distances with a trained eye, but with the understanding and knowledge of these rules of perspective.

Figs. 187 and 187A (above, left). A formula to divide a space in perspective to determine its center.

Fig. 182 to 184 (opposite page). The horizon line is situated directly ahead of us at eye level as we look ahead.

Figs. 188 to 192 (below). Formula to divide a space to describe depth and perspective.

189

190

191

192

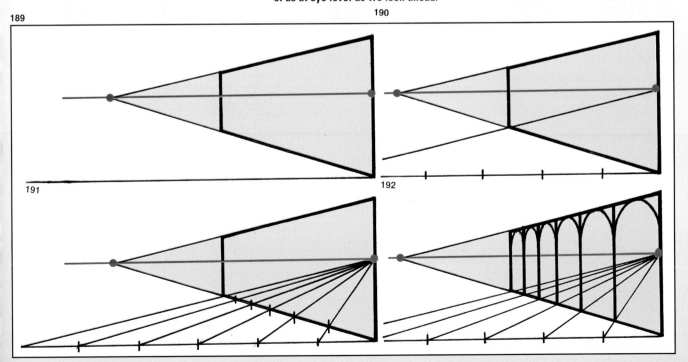

Basic Perspective, Guide Lines

193

Painting an urban landscape, a street or a house, you would generally use oblique perspective and you may well find that the vanishing point is found outside the perimeter of the painting, as in the example set out here (fig. 193). Once again let me remind you that the experienced artist sketches and paints by eye, simply drawing what he sees, however, in order to understand the logic and to establish the perspective accurately you can use a system of guide lines, following the process set out in the adjoining images (figs. 194-196). It is straightforward, you can try it out right now in order to understand it better.

194

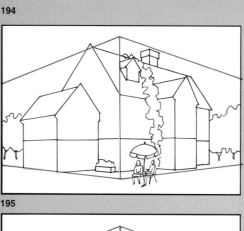

Fig. 193. Painting subjects such as this in perspective, where the vanishing points fall outside of the picture plane. You can either estimate where the lines would converge by eye, alternatively you can use a guideline as explained in the following diagrams.

195

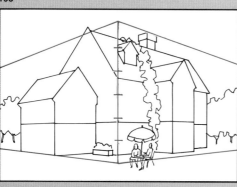

196

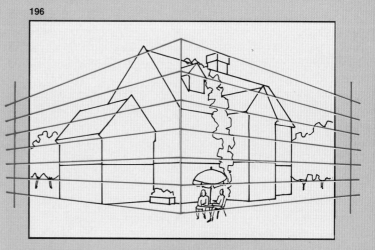

Fig. 194 (above). Box in the building drawing a vertical through the point nearest the viewer (A), and trace lines B and C by eye and in perspective which frame the top and the base of the subject to be drawn.

Fig. 195. Divide the vertical (A) into a number of equal parts, six in this case.

Fig. 196. Outside the picture's limit in the left-hand margin, draw another vertical and divide it into six equal parts.

Do the same on the right. Now join the points to form the lines (D, E, F, etc.) heading towards the vanishing points on both sides to form the guidelines.

Atmosphere: Additional Perspective

There is another form of perspective, it has no lines or vanishing points, no division of space, but it also recreates a third dimension, that of depth, which is the aim of all types of perspective.

This is the perspective created by atmosphere which causes a contrast between the definition of the foreground and the diffusion and fading of color in the distant horizon. This effect was commonly used by Leonardo da Vinci and referred to in his *Treatise on Painting*:

"You must give the foreground a detailed finish, the middle ground should be less detailed and in succession the recession of distance, the outlines become less defined, objects shapes and colors merge and fade".

This statement was reiterated by Cézanne, the same sentiment expressed in a different way, when he wrote from Aix to another painter, Emile Bernard:

"For us artists, Nature is more about depth than about surface, this means that we have to introduce into the light that we capture a sufficient amount of blues to recreate the sense of the air's atmosphere".

This effect is present, in the subject, in nature, in a landscape or seascape pictured against the light or in an idealized image when the artist introduces a sort of misty effect created by the sun and the depth of the scene and which serves to capture the perspective (fig. 197).

Bear this in mind and try to capture this sort of light to accentuate aerial perspective of atmosphere, the third dimension.

Fig. 197. Joseph Mallord William Turner (1775-1851). *The Grand Canal with the Church of Santa Maria della Salute.* Tate Gallery, London. This is a Romantic interpretation of the Grand Canal in Venice, in which Turner illustrates this principle of perspective using atmospheric effects captured by the contrast of the gondolas, the scene has been embellished but you can make out the church of Santa Maria and the rest of the buildings in an undefined mass amongst the blues and grays of the atmospheric haze.

How to Select your Subject

I am a great admirer of the Impressionists, Monet, Cézanne and particularly Van Gogh. I find Monet's life and works very moving, his early years were a desperate struggle, he worked slavishly –spending two years retouching and revising his series of studies on Rouen Cathedral– when his art dealer requested additional studies for the same price. I admire and envy Cézanne for never being satisfied with himself, *"I am incapable of expressing this magnificent richness of color which enlivens nature"*, he wrote to his son from Aix, despite unwittingly being one of the key protagonists of modern art of the twentieth century.

I am particularly drawn to Van Gogh, by his work, his life and his madness. I think that an important lesson lies in the history of his life, for example, when, having lost his reason a year before committing suicide, he discovered color and light and painted the best works of his entire life.

He wrote to his brother Théo from the Hospital of Sant Remy, *"Since I've been in this place with its unkempt garden, planted with big pine trees with grass growing high and wild at their foot, I have plenty of material to work with"*.

For Van Gogh a deserted garden (fig. 199) was a perfect subject to paint, as was a chair (fig. 200) or the dormitory in Arles where he was before he went into hospital (fig. 198). Van Gogh, like Monet and Cézanne, was a fervent admirer of the painter Eugéne Delacroix. He wrote this in his diary:

The subject is yourself, your impressions, your emotions when face to face with Nature.

198

199

Figs. 198 and 199. Vincent van Gogh (1853-1890). *Ward of the Hospital.* Oskar Reinhart collection, Winterthur, Switzerland. And *Malez. The Garden.* Rijksmuseum, Amsterdam. In May 1889, Van Gogh was interned once more at Saint Rémy Hospital. He was given two rooms, one to sleep in and another to work in. In his first days there he was too scared to go out of the hospital and he painted the bedroom or what he could see from his window. This was how he came to paint the unkempt garden; this was the favourite painting of the wife of his brother, Théo.

Fig. 200. Vincent van Gogh. *Van Gogh's chair.* National Gallery, London. Van Gogh painted ano-ther chair, *Gauguin's chair,* he was living with Gauguin for some months before they fell out. Gauguin's chair was an expensive, upholstered chair, while Van Gogh's chair was a basic and crude, with a rush seat.

Selecting a Subject

200

201

202

203

Fig. 201. Vincent van Gogh. *Summer evening, sunset over a wheat field.* Kunstmuseum, Winterthur. Van Gogh wrote that he had finished painting the picture in a single afternoon in an attempt to capture the violence of the mistral.

Fig. 202. Claude Monet (1840-1926). *The Seine at Argenteuil.* Museum of Modern Art, San Francisco. The river Seine once again, with its tree lined banks and the dappled light and shadows, the sky dotted with

clouds of different sizes; a motif that Monet painted when living in Argenteuil, in Vetheuil and in Giverny.

Fig. 203. Paul Cézanne (1839-1906). *Poor man's house.* Musée d'Orsay, Paris. Painted in 1873 this painting was exhibited a the first Impressionist Exhibition which opened on 15 April 1874 on the premises of Nadar, a photographer, at 35 Boulevard des Capucines, Paris.

What the Impressionists Chose to Paint

When Paul Cézanne was painting in L'Estaque, a small village set on the shores of the gulf of Marseilles (fig. 204), he wrote to his son Lucien: *"Subjects multiply here, the same theme seen from a different angle presents me with such a different scene that I could work and paint for months without so much as moving from this spot, simply turning my head a little to the right or a little to the left".*

A story, while we're talking about choosing a theme or a subject to paint: the famous North American watercolorist John Singer Sargent (1856-1925) organized an excursion along the Thames in 1885 with a group of artist friends including the poet Edmund Gosse who described how the American artist found a subject to paint, *"He took along his enormous easel, walking along in the open air he would suddenly set himself down in a random place, behind a barn, by a wall, in the middle of a field... his aim being to reproduce whatever he saw there"* (fig. 205).

De Liebermann, (1847-1935) the most important German Impressionist once commented *"it is all the same to me whether I paint a rose or a virgin".*

From these comments you may well conclude that choosing your subject matter is relatively easy. There are a choice of subjects from your own house; roofs and roof terraces, to the streets and squares of towns that you live in or visit; the fields and woodland, garden, beach or any area that you know.

"Subjects, motifs?" said Renoir, *"I solve that problem with the first thing that falls my way!"*

That is all very well but Cézanne, Sargent and Renoir –all Impressionists in fact–, certainly made clear their indifference for the subject matter, their paintings featured unremarkable subjects such as a river with four sailing boats (fig. 206), a group of workmen mending the road (fig. 207), a busy square full of people, horses, and carriages viewed from a balcony (fig. 208) or the terrace of a café at night (fig. 209). Although they chose these sort of scenes to paint, it is definite that they had seen merit in them. They had analyzed the subject as suitable for a formal composition, with chromatic value and they had imagined beforehand how they were going to interpret it.

The selection of a motif or subject to paint depends on an understanding of three factors:

1. **Vision**
2. **Composition**
3. **Interpretation**

Which means studying the subject or landscape and considering as you do so the best format, the best light, the best view point, the formal structure of the work and the color range. The composition needs to be considered and analyzed; which details should be left out or enhanced, the color that will dominate the image and the contrasts that can be accentuated. This is how you achieve "introspection", how you will be interpreting the image.

204

Fig. 204. Paul Cézanne. *The gulf of L'Estaque.* **Chicago Institute of Art, collection of Mr & Mrs Martin A. Ryerson. This was one of Cézanne's favourite places where, as he said** *"I believe that I could stay in the same place for months without moving".* **He painted four large paintings of L'Estaque. Look carefully at the contrasts that have been enhanced, such as the lighter patches on the sea in the foreground, the center of the bay and the dark borders outlining the mountains on the left in the background.**

205

206

Fig. 205 (opposite page). John Singer Sargent (1856-1925). *Fire on the mountain.* The Brooklyn Museum, Brooklyn. A highly skilled oil painter, Sargent was famous for his magnificent portraits which were reminiscent of the style of Velázquez, with the influence of Manet and Courbet. John Singer Sargent was also a remarkable watercolorist, considered one of the best of the beginning of the century.

Fig. 206. Claude Monet (1840-1926). *Regattas in Argenteuil.* Musée d'Orsay, Paris. Have a good look at this landscape and you will notice that the contrasts are created by color alone, there is no use of light and shade, demonstrating, as Bonnard said, that *"Color alone can describe the shapes of objects".* This is a good example of colorist painting which we will discuss later on.

207

209

208

Fig. 207. Edouard Manet (1832-1883). *Workmen in Rue Mosnier.* Fitzwilliam Museum, Cambridge. This painting was painted in 1878. For people of that time it seemed inconceivable and ridiculous to paint subjects so trivial as workmen paving the street.

Fig. 208. Camille Pissarro (1831-1903). *La Place du Théâtre de Paris.* Hermitage Museum, St. Petersburg. Urban landscape was restored as an artistic subject by the Impressionists.

Fig. 209. Vincent van Gogh (1853-1890). *Terrace of the café in the Place du Forum.* Rijksmuseum Kröller-Muller, Otterlo. A wonderful choice of subject, look at the dramatic color contrasts created by the juxtaposition of the yellow with the intense blue.

How Monet Painted

210

211

212

Monet was born in Paris in 1840 and died in 1926. As a child he used to go to Le Havre with his parents where he made a name for himself drawing caricatures which he sometimes exhibited along with landscapes painted by a painter called Eugene Boudin. Monet said "One day Boudin said to me, 'You are a talented artist, why don't you dedicate yourself to landscape painting?' ". Monet (fig. 210) took his advice and painted his first landscapes near the estuary of the river Seine. The Seine, which cuts through the center of Paris and meets the sea at Le Havre (fig. 211), played a major role in Monet's work. He never lived far from its banks; seven years in Argenteuil, just over three years in Vetheuil and twenty seven years in Giverny next to the river Epte, a tributary of the Seine.

He worked untiringly, he always had various different canvases in progress at any one time. *"I work like a madman, painting six canvases a day"*, he wrote from Bordighera (Italy). And from Giverny, on his return from Bordighera he wrote to Durand-Ruel, his art dealer, *"I have worked without rest for three months, in a state of anguish and dissatisfaction about the paintings I have produced"*.

Did he work slowly? No, it was just that many of his paintings started out as sketches made outdoors which he then converted into paintings in his studio. He was a perfectionist, he would paint, repaint, scrub out and restart. He wrote about the Water-lily series (fig. 212) to his art dealer Durand-Ruel *"I cannot exhibit the Water-lily series this year because I only have five or six decent canvases, I have just destroyed*

213

Fig. 210 (opposite page, top left). Claude Monet (1840-1926). *Self portrait.* Musée d'Orsay, Paris. Monet painted this self portrait in 1917, when he was living in Giverny, his time absorbed by his water garden and the lengthy Water-lily series.

Fig. 211 (opposite page). Claude Monet. *Impression, Sunrise.* As you may already know, this was the picture that Monet entered for the first Impressionist exhibition in 1874. Leroy, an art critic attempted to make a mockery of the picture's title and from his article the name of this art form, "Impressionism", was born.

214

about thirty of them which was most satisfying".

In another letter to Alice he wrote, "I have come home from work, it was unconstructive. I have wiped out all that I did this morning".

In 1890 he started a series of paintings taking the same theme and painting it at different hours during the day, to study the different effects of light and shade. In the first, the haystack series (fig. 213) he painted 16 paintings which met with great approval when exhibited by Durand-Ruel. This encouraged him to work on 15 paintings, the poplar series (fig. 214), then followed a series on the Gare Saint Lazare and later, from 1892 to 1893 he painted his famous series, the Cathedrals, followed by the widely acclaimed Water-lily series. These latter two series are considered his most important.

Fig. 212 (opposite page). Claude Monet. *The lake at Giverny.* Museum of Painting and Sculpture, Grenoble. This picture, painted in 1917, belongs to a period when Monet had been through a great learning curve of experience; color, contrasts, composition and interpretation, which gave him the ability to see and capture the scene with extraordinary skill.

Fig. 213 (above). Claude Monet. *Haystacks.* Musée d'Orsay, Paris. Monet painted 16 canvases in this series. He was observed leaving Giverny early in the morning, accompanied by a helper with barrow containing various canvases so that he could paint the same haystack at different times of day, observing the effects of the changing light, color and contrasts.

Fig. 214. Claude Monet. *Poplars on the river Epte.* National Gallery of Scotland, Edinburgh. Monet's life long fascination for water is evident in the Poplar series, admire the reflections in the water and the format with the crowns of the trees forming a graceful curve that is reflected in the water.

How Monet Painted

One of the most beautiful cathedrals in the whole of France belongs to the city of Rouen, in the North East of France on the river Seine. Monet decided to paint a number of canvases which featured the passage of the sun across the Cathedral's facade (fig. 215 & 216). He rented a premises opposite the facade and for a number of months worked there intensely, swapping from one canvas to another as the direction and conditions of the light altered. He painted almost fifty canvases in total. *"I get up before six and work until half past seven in the evening, on my feet all that time, nine canvases, it's killing me"*. When he finished the series he returned to his home in Giverny and spent nearly two years retouching and altering the fifty paintings of the series.

The last series that Monet painted was the Water-lilies, which he started on in 1909. In the garden of his house in Giverny, Monet created a water garden by diverting water from the river Epte, forming a little Japanese style lake full of water-lilies surrounded by weeping willows. Monet worked in his garden for more than twenty years, painting flowers and leaves of water-lilies with the sky and the clouds reflected in the water of the lake (fig. 217). The result was a gigantic collection of about 250 works, these included 19 panels, two metres high, of different lengths which Monet left

to the French state at the request of his great friend, and then president of the French Republic, Georges Clemenceau. Today, this series decorates the Orangerie in the Tullerie Gardens in Paris. But how did Monet paint? A section of the painting in figure 219 is reproduced in detail on the following pages (80-81).

Read the commentary alongside this which explains Monet's language, his workmanship and technique in this

Figs. 215 & 216. Claude Monet. *Rouen Cathedral, morning sun*. Musée d'Orsay, Paris, and *Rouen Cathedral*, Metropolitan Museum of Art, Washington. Here are two examples of the Cathedral series, the first (fig. 215), painted in the blazing sunshine using extraordinary contrasts and impasto, and the second with a more diffuse light which subtly contrasts with the other.

Fig. 217. Claude Monet. *The clouds*. Oil on canvas 2 m x 12.75 m. Musée de l'Orangerie, Paris. This is one of the 19 panels that Monet painted and left to the French state.

painting, and consider the following facts:

Colors used by Monet. Monet himself wrote in a letter to his dealer, Durand-Ruel about the colors he used, *"The trick is to use basic colors. The choice is a matter of habit. Basically I use silver white, cadmium yellow, vermilion, deep madder, cobalt blue and emerald green and that is all"* (fig. 218).

Working in the open air he would paint in a housecoat and he would use a sunshade to protect himself from the glare of the sun, to avoid being dazzled, which makes you paint with darker colors. On the Seine, in Argenteuil, he converted a boat into a floating studio, he used to paint in the boat so that he could study the reflections and colors of the waters during different times of day.

He would paint his landscapes in various different sessions. In one of his letters he talks of 22 sessions in one single landscape, and this allowed him to paint with light, *impasto* colors applied over dry paint. He always painted outdoors, but never gave up retouching his work in his studio.

He painted with a free hand and large "comma" brushstrokes.

In the following pages you will see the commentary on Monet's techniques and study a detail of the painting below (fig. 219).

218

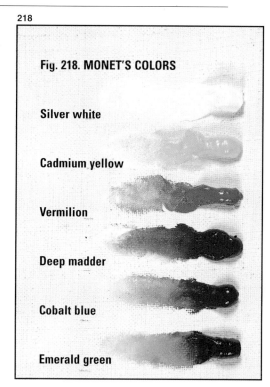

Fig. 218. MONET'S COLORS

Silver white

Cadmium yellow

Vermilion

Deep madder

Cobalt blue

Emerald green

219

Fig. 219. Claude MONET. *View of Vethuil in Summer.* 100 cm x 65 cm. Metropolitan Museum of Art, New York. Have a look at how Monet painted in the following pages, a detail of this painting, approximately half the size of the original is explained with the help of adjoining text.

How Monet Painted

Fig. 220. Claude Monet. *View of Vetheuil in Summer* **(detail). 100 cm x 65 cm. Metropolitan Museum of Art, New York. Here are some detailed observations about Monet's approach to painting:**

1. He painted with his eyes half closed. If you half close your eyes and look at this reproduction from a certain distance you will see the subject as Monet saw it, the little details practically disappear, forms are simplified and contrasts are accentuated.

2. He painted in various sessions. This is evident from the clouds in the sky (cobalt blue, darker above, lighter towards the horizon), the white paint with a touch of yellow, is applied on top of the blue, looking at the brush marks you can see that it was applied on top of dry paint. This is even clearer when you study the reflections of the houses in the waters of the Seine.

3. He painted with sweeping brush-strokes in the shape of a comma. It is almost certain he used a number 12 brush for the large brushstrokes of the clouds and a number 8 flat hog's hair brush for the comma-like marks used on the water for the reflections, and a number 8 flat sable brush for outlining the crowns of the trees, the windows and for defining the houses.

4. He painted with layers of *impasto.* i.e. with various layers of thick paint which were overlaid, sometimes on wet but nearly always on dry and normally with a slight variation of color between the different coats. You will see this if you look at the bell tower and the houses, and particularly the houses' reflections on the water. Study the way Monet paints the water, initially he painted various layers with hardly any impasto but with many hints of different colors (have a look on the left, under the trees), and then he developed the reflections by adding impasto with light colored paint on top.

220

How Turner Painted

221

Joseph Mallord William Turner (fig. 221) showed his talent from a very early age. He was born in Maiden Lane, Covent Garden in London. He was the son of a barber, his mother died when he was very young and his talent for drawing and painting became evident when he was still only a child. When he was only nine years old he was given etchings to color; his father gave up being a barber and dedicated his life to helping his son, living with him until his death. Turner was apprenticed to Thomas Malton's studio and this was his introduction to watercolor landscape painting. His understanding of perspective is already evident (fig. 222). Afterwards, as a student of the Royal Academy, his works already demonstrated the qualities of a watercolor expert, and he was only 16 years old! His skill is evident in his choice of subject matter, the format, color harmonies, the atmosphere and perspective which all demonstrated his remarkable capacity which put him on a level with the most talented professional artists of his era. It is hardly surprising that one of his watercolors, Interior of Tintern Abbey, Monmouthshire (fig. 223) was exhibited in 1794 in the annual exhibition of the Royal Academy. As I mentioned previously, he was finally elected as an Associate member of the Royal Academy at the age of 26 and some years later he was nominated President.

In 1792 when he was 27, Turner made one of his

Fig. 221. Joseph Mallord William Turner (1775-1851). *Self portrait.* Tate Gallery, London.

Fig. 222. Turner. *Church of Christ, Merton Fields.* British Museum, London. At 16, Turner was painting watercolors like this one, using colors in much the same way as his master Thomas Malton, whose style had a great influence on Turner at that time.

Fig. 223. Turner. *Interior of Tintern Abbey, Monmouthshire.* Tate Gallery, London. This is the watercolor that Turner presented which was exhibited in 1794 in the Annual Exhibition of the Royal Academy. Turner had visited the ruins of Tintern Abbey two years previously, in 1792 and had made a number of pencil sketches with which he prepared this painting in his studio. It is, as you can see, an impressive demonstration of his skill in perspective.

222

223

first trips outside of London. From this time he began the practice of drawing pencil sketches from life. These would later be transformed into watercolor paintings in the studio. He continued with this practice throughout his life, except on a few occasions when he would paint an entire painting outdoors, directly from nature. It was perfectly normal for him to be working on a number of watercolors and oils in the studio at the same time, alternating from one to the other.

For three years, from 1794, Turner became part of a group of watercolorists including Girtin, Cotman, Varley, Cox and De Wint among others, who gathered in Doctor Monro's house to hone their skills by copying sketches and watercolor works of famous artists, above all John Robert Cozens (1752-1797), who was a patient of Dr Monro. Those three years of study with Girtin and his peers, with the knowledge he gained from his exposure to the works of J.R. Cozens, were a rich period of assimilation and discovery about watercolor techniques (fig. 224). One should also add that it was during his third year of studies at Dr Monro's that Turner started painting in oils. In 1796 he exhibited his first oils in the Royal Academy.

Fig. 224. Turner. *The houses of Parliament burning*. British Museum, London. Turner painted nine watercolors of this subject in his studio, based on a series of pencil sketches. This famous watercolor is a masterclass of realism, technique and synthesis, with very few forms and a narrow range of colors.

How Turner Painted

225

226

Not only was Turner a skilled craftsman of watercolor he was a great master of oil painting as well. This talent for different media can also be admired in other artists such as Dürer, Jordaens, Bonington, Fortuny, Sargent, Sorolla, Hopper, Seago, etc. There is no doubt that the mastery of two different media was very beneficial for all these artists. And Turner saw the benefits when he started to master the skills of oil painting. From that moment Turner started to paint his watercolors on tinted paper, dyed gray, blue or cream, etc. on which he would paint his subject, relying considerably on the use of white gouache (fig. 225). This broadened and developed his skills beyond the techniques of pure watercolor.

He had the ability to draw and paint from memory, developing and inventing forms and colors and incorporating moving figures developed from simple drawings observed from nature (fig. 226). He broke away from the affected style adopted by the painters of ruins and topographical landscapes, works whose principal merits were that they appeared as an exact copy of the model through application of the rules of perspective. Turner's freedom of imagination exasperated his critics who considered his works "vulgar, crude and disorganized."

The painter William Leighton Leitch told his student James Orrock some particulars about Turners techniques, "He would work on a number of watercolors at the same time. He started by submerging the sheet of paper in a water bath, then he would spread the sheet on a board and apply the tones for the sky and the background while the paper was still damp, painting in subtle gradations. Once these washes were dry, he would paint over them, applying paint and describing shapes at an incredible pace". This process was definitely used with one of the most famous watercolors painted by Turner on his last trip to Venice in 1840, *San Giorgio Maggiore from the Aduana. Daybreak* (fig. 227). The famous English critic Ruskin –a staunch defender of Turner– commented in his book, *Modern Painters*, on the special techniques such as, *"the use of his thumbnail especially to lift off white spaces, scratching at newly painted areas, and the use of saliva mixed in with color. Occasionally he would substitute a nail for the pointed end of his paintbrush with which he would lift off white spaces"*. Ruskin also referred to a treatment that Turner had for the backgrounds of some of his watercolors: *"Having painted the forms in the background such as the houses, buildings or mountains in the more distant planes of the picture he would sometimes submerge the paper in a water bath in order to soften the outlines and create atmosphere. To make this even more effective he would turn the sheet of paper around on the wooden board and with the tip of his thumb he pressed down on the wet paint, smudging the patches where he wanted to lessen the definition"*.

227

Fig. 225 (opposite page). Turner. *The source of the river Arveiron.* Tate Gallery, London. Landscape painted in 1802, using a mixed technique which, as well as a gray wash to tint the paper, he used lead pencil, watercolor, highlights in white gouache, scratching to lift off white spaces using his thumbnail, over the area representing a wood (you can see the scratches in the brown mountain on the left, above the white area).

Fig. 226 (opposite page). Turner. *Whitby.* Tate Gallery, London. Whitby is a port that Turner painted as one of the serie "Ports of England". Whitby earned great praise from the critic John Ruskin. This watercolor is based on a few basic sketches to which Turner added the boats and the figures, painted from memory.

Fig. 227. Turner. *Venice. San Giorgio Maggiore from the Aduana.* British Museum, London. You will see this watercolor reproduced in original size (22.4 cm x 28.7 cm) in the two following pages, along with some observations about how Turner painted.

228

FIG. 228. TURNER'S COLORS

Cadmium yellow medium   Emerald green

Raw sienna   Sepia

Cadmium red   Ultramarine blue

Madder carmine   Ivory black

There is no reference in existence about the selection of colors that Turner used, however, we have information about the palette of his friend Thomas Girtin (fig. 228).

On the following pages there is a life-sized reproduction of the painting *San Giorgio Maggiore from the Aduana* (fig. 227), with a series of observations rounding off this overview about how Turner painted.

How Turner Painted

Fig. 229. Turner. *Venice. San Giorgio Maggiore from the Aduana.* 22.4 cm x 28.7 cm. British Museum, London. Reproduced in its original size, the same size that it was painted by Turner. Have a look at the observations about Turner's approach to watercolor.

1. The first step. A wash of color on wet. First, Turner wet the entire sheet of paper with water and then he painted on wet; a very delicate gray wash made up of a light gray with a hint of yellow to give it a warm tone. This was applied with a thick brush. This color was intensified a little in the foreground and then he opened a white space in the foreground on the left with a fine clean brush.

2. There are no pencil sketch marks. There are no traces of pencil marks or drawing. Turner painted this watercolor straight from nature, he had no need of any reference points or sketching as he was right in front of the scene.

3. Describing the buildings. Let's focus on the church of San Giorgio Maggiore; first Turner painted a general wash of gray with a hint of rose which he applied to the facade of the buildings, leaving the highlighted areas in yellow on the left-hand side of the building and the two patches on the right. With this same pinkish gray he painted the tower, the cupola and the houses on the right, including the roofs. In the center, below the cupola he made the pinkish gray deeper. He waited until the rose gray background was dry and then, with black, a touch of cobalt blue and plenty of water he described the tower the cupola and the roofs. This gray color is lighter on the cupola and on the roofs of the houses on the right, and once dry, Turner overpainted the gray on the roofs of the those houses as you can see on the edge of the penultimate gray roof.

4. The strips of land in the center and on the left. With this same pinkish gray color and a soft grayish blue on his brush, it seems that Turner then painted the delicate spits extending into the sea; the quayside that extends from San Giorgio Maggiore in the center and the other strip, on the left in the distance. He added the boats near the strips of land at the same time.

5. The boats on the right in the middle distance. I am fairly certain that Turner painted these boats before adding the gray reflections of the tower in the water. This would explain why the boats appear to be painted onto the yellowish background. I also wonder if Turner invented them or painted them from memory. I wondered this because that would explain how Turner forgot to include the reflections of the masts in the water. Whatever the case, these boats are an impressive example of synthesis and watercolor technique.

6. The reflections. It is very likely that in reality the reflections were far stronger, they would have been sharper and more visible. However, Turner interpreted them like this, with a few light gray brushstrokes in which you can just make out the reflection of the tower. Although I do wonder, should he have painted more forms and introduced more colors which would detract from the luminosity of the water? No, I think not. The beauty and merit of this watercolor, one of the most breathtaking in the history of watercolor, is the luminosity and simplicity of the format. Turner has interpreted this scene with consummate skill.

229

Fig. 230. José M. Parramón (b.1919). *The Port of Genoa* (detail). Private collection. There is no strict format determining the artistic composition of this watercolor, neither does it adhere to the rule of the golden section. It does work however. It could be that the tug, its coloring, and its shading, defines a foreground from which the depth of the picture can develop; it could be that the shapes and colors of the tug and the ship behind create a mass that gives a solidity to the format, or it could be the diversity of the colors in general. Either way, I think that this watercolor is a good example of composition and interpretation.

COMPOSITION AND INTERPRETATION OF LANDSCAPE

In 1837 the editor Walter William, director of
Architectural Magazine, commissioned an article from
John Ruskin on the rules of composition. A couple of
days later Ruskin handed in a document consisting of a
few lines, *"There are no rules on the art of composition. If
it were possible to compose a painting by simply
adhering to rules, Titian and Veronese would have been
average, unremarkable human beings"*. Well, that is a
thought. It is true that there are no absolute rules on the
art of composition –art is not an exact science– but there
are a series of precedents and principles which will help
you to develop your creative capacities, make you more
artistically aware, and transform your perception from
that of the average person to that of someone who
understands art and aesthetics. This is what we will be
looking at in the following pages which are full of graphic
examples demonstrating the art of composition
and interpretation of landscape.

Unity within Variety

Fig. 231 The Greek philosopher, Plato.

Many words have been written on the subject of the art of composition, from the definition of Henri Matisse:

"Composition is the art of decoratively arranging the distinct elements that the painter has at his disposal in order to express himself."

And Cézanne who commented:

"Painting is the art of combining effects, in other words, establishing relations between colors, contours and planes."

Or the thoughts of Jean Guitton the teacher who said:

"Composition is the search for equilibrium and proportion, thus achieving beauty."

232 A

That is all very well, but the art student asks, how do I achieve this "art of decoratively arranging the distinct elements that are at the artist's disposal?"

What and where are these elements?

The Greek philosopher, Plato (fig. 231) answered these questions by establishing the following rule:

Composition is the discovery and representation of Unity within Variety.

With this norm in mind René Huyghe, the honorary director of the Louvre and author of the book *Dialogue with Art* developed the idea that it could be dangerous to endeavour to shape Unity. If you are too demanding the result will negatively affect the concept of the work. And, he added *"At the very least you have to enrich this Unity by developing Diversity."*

Let's say for example that you demonstrate diversity or variety through color, shape, position, size and arrangement of the elements of the landscape. When this diversity exists the picture's viewer will be attracted by its composition; this variety captures their attention and maintains their interest.

But beware! This variety cannot be so exaggerated that the viewer's attention is distracted by the various elements of interest. Huyghe's suggestion is therefore very accurate, you must combine both factors in such a way that any landscape contains both elements:

**Unity within variety
Variety within unity**

This balance between unity and variety depends on other factors,
**Vary the format to introduce Unity more effectively through:
A: Better organization
B: Adaptation of the theme to a geometrically structured format
Variety within unity can be achieved by
A: Dramatizing the contrasts of tone and color
B: Enhancing textures**

Cézanne's painting (figs. 232 & 232A) exemplifies the effective application of Unity within Variety.

Fig. 232. Paul Cézanne. *Landscape, Nature study*. Private collection, Switzerland. This is a good example of Plato's norm, demonstrated by the schematic diagram (fig. 232A). Fig. 232A. Shows how the factor of Unity is obtained through the inclusion of a strong diagonal (red line) into the format, while Cézanne has balanced it with the effect of Variety through the diversity of tones and colors. What is more, Cézanne strengthened the composition even more by applying the rule of the golden section (red line on the horizon).

232

Format and Composition. The Golden Rule

You have arrived at "the scene of the crime". You saw this landscape a few days ago and now you set down your easel, set up the canvas, set out your palette and... Wait a second! Have you thought about the schematic composition? Have you established if the image follows a precise geometric format? Also consider if there is a horizon or a central motif, a focus, perhaps a farmhouse or a village. Have you considered the possibility of altering the format, bringing the horizon up or down so that the focus of the image coincides with the grid of Euclid's Golden Section? What is this Golden Section of Euclid's? I will explain presently, but first let me point out that in the art of composition there is one factor of decisive importance, the format of the scene. *"...By altering the angle from which you portray the subject you can transform it into a far more interesting scene"*, Cézanne said to Lucien, his son. This is of crucial importance and bears repeating.

Format and composition are one.

Now I will explain the Golden Section. In the third century B. C. famous mathematician lived a in Greek Alexandria. Euclid was the author of a number of works including one called Elements. In volume IV of this work, Euclid studied the aesthetics of proportions and established an ideal division of a line or any given space. Fifteen centuries later, during the Renaissance, Luca Pacioli, the most famous mathematician of the fifteenth century discovered the work by Euclid and wrote the book *Divina Proportione*, which was illustrated by Leonardo da Vinci, in which he developed Euclid's formulas, labelling them as the Golden Rule, the Golden Point and the Golden Section. The following text and diagrams give an explanation and a demonstration of the use of the Golden Section, taking Van Gogh's landscape, *Wheat fields under stormy skies* (figs. 233, 234 &

235), a landscape to which Van Gogh applied the rule of the Golden Section. On the following pages we will discuss to what extent this format coincided with a schematic plan for creating unity.

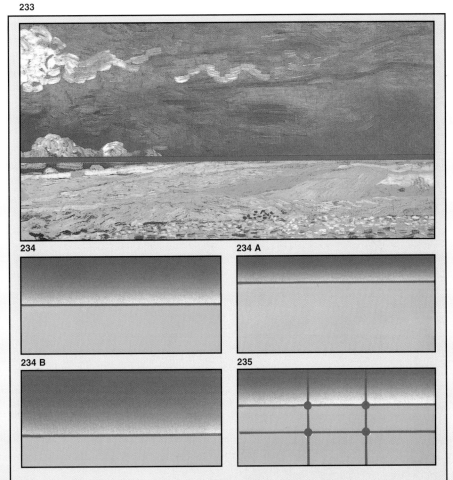

233

234   234 A

234 B   235

The Law of the Golden Section

Figs. 233, 234 and 235. In the painting *Wheat fields under stormy skies*, Van Gogh could have situated his horizon level in the center of the picture (fig. 234), or in the upper part of the canvas (fig. 234A), or in the lower part of the canvas (fig. 234B). Instead Van Gogh situated the horizon in the ideal place (fig. 233, top.), because he knew the Rule of the Golden Section which goes as follows:

For any given space divided into unequal parts, the most pleasing and aesthetic result will be obtained if there is the same relation between the smaller and the larger part as there is between the larger part and the whole.

To achieve this ideal division, all you have to do is multiply the height or the width of the canvas by 0.618. If you do this multiplication sum for height and width you will arrive at a set of golden points or focal points, the ideal places to situate the key motif of the picture. This point can be situated in one of four points as indicated in figure 235.

The Format as a Factor of Unity

By using the Law of the Golden Section we have arranged the pictorial space and highlighted the subject's focal point. Now we need to consider how to find a format that obeys a particular geometrical arrangement to reinforce the impression of unity. But, how do you go about finding that format? And why does it need to be geometrical?

It has been established that human beings, when told to choose between different forms, prefer geometrical shapes. This fact was proven by a German philosopher called Fechner, who studied the relations between physical and psychological phenomena of shapes. Fechner gave a large group of people a card which featured natural shapes, geometrical shapes and abstract shapes (fig. 236); he then asked which of these groups of shapes were the most pleasing, the most harmonious and which they liked the most; the answers demonstrated that *"the best shapes, those which catch*

artistic compositions. They have immense prestige". wrote Huyghe. This use of geometric shapes appears already in Renaissance works in which the triangle predominates (figs. 237 & 237A). In the Baroque period much use was made of the diagonal composition (figs. 238 & 238A). Apart from these formats, now considered "classical" formats, and other traditional formats such as the rectangle, square and oval; formats based on typographical shapes such as L, C, Z, etc. are also popular. You will see some examples of these sorts of compositions in the images by famous artists on the opposite page (figs. 239, 240, 241 & 242).

Studying these images and the corresponding diagrams illustrating their formats clearly demonstrates that the format is one of the most important elements for creating Unity in the picture and, as a consequence it holds the composition together.

If you can identify a particular format

in a landscape that you are about to paint, try to enhance it, even if it means having to modify, suppress or exaggerate certain elements. Bear in mind the rule **format is composition**, and always consider how you could vary the viewpoint, constantly looking for an alternative composition in which the landscape presents you with a ready determined format.

Fig. 236. The German philosopher Fechner proved by using this diagram that people asked to choose between abstract, natural and geometric shapes, prefer the last of these.

Fig. 237 & 238. Raphael (1483-1520). *The Holy Family with Saint Anne and Saint John.* **Alta Pinacoteca, Monaco. Rubens (1577-1640).** *Charity.* **Pommers Felden, Schlos Weissenstein, Schönborn collection. Renaissance and Baroque artists were already using geometrical forms as the formats for composition.**

236

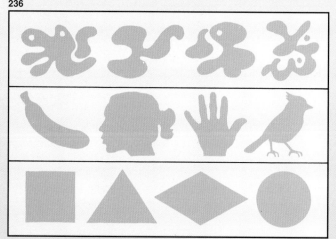

the attention and which are remembered most easily are geometric shapes".

Justifying this simple and proven preference, the theoreticians were of the opinion that *"The evident mesmerizing power of certain shapes and shape combinations is a consequence of the theory of hedonism: to obtain the maximum satisfaction with the minimum effort or the principal of muscular, nervous or mental economy"*, wrote C. R. Haas. The results of Fechner's experiments appear to be substantiated in many paintings by artists who used geometric shapes in the composition of their works. *" The circle, the square and the triangle are present in the format of many*

237

237 A

238

238 A

239

239 A

241 A

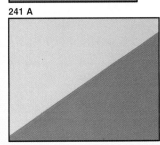

Fig. 239. Paul Cézanne (1839-1906). *View of L'Estaque through the trees*. Private collection. Cézanne enhanced the depth by leaving the foreground undefined and by using yellows and reds which brings the houses in the middle ground closer in contrast with the blue of the sea.

Fig. 239. Moreover, Cézanne built a format into the composition which reinforces the unity of the picture; if you also consider the variety of colors and shapes you can admire this masterpiece of composition.

Figs. 240 & 240A. Trevor Chamberlain. *September morning in Stainthes*. By courtesy of the editorial David & Charles, London. Chamberlain has created an excellent watercolor, constructing the format in a reversed L shape which strengthens the Unity of the composition.

240

241

240 A

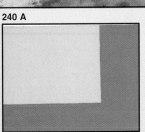

242 A

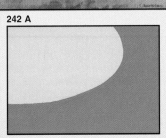

242

Figs. 241 & 241A. Edward Hopper (1882-1967). *Le Quai des Grands Agustins*. Whitney Museum of American Art, New York. Hopper, an American artist, was in Paris in 1909 when he painted this work with a diagonal format.

Figs. 242 & 242A. Camille Pissarro (1831-1903). *The Seine at Marly*. Belonging to R. Peto, Paris. Pissarro constructed this image of the Seine, giving it a format that compliments the composition.

Variety through Contrast and Texture

Contrast of tones, contrast of color and texture, three factors that can be varied to create Variety within Unity, catching the viewer's attention, awakening their interest.

The English watercolorist John Yardley (b. 1933) presents us with a perfect example of a painting that catches the attention and awakens the interest because of its excellent technique and its extraordinary use of tone and contrast which provide Variety in the composition of his *Facade of St Mark's, in Venice*.

As a contrast to this exceptional watercolor, have a look at the figure 244, an oil painting by Joaquim Mir where he has used a range of the complementary colors orange and blue a contrast which is further emphasized by the dark foreground. Together these factors create an excellent example of Variety (fig. 244A).

This variety through contrast is also a factor used by Maurice Prendergast, an American watercolorist (1859-1924). He was born in Boston, and travelled to England in 1886 and to Paris five years later, where he met Manet and Whistler. On his third voyage to Europe in 1898, he visited Venice where he painted a number of watercolors

such as figure 245. Typical of his work, the scene has a bustling atmosphere created by the passers by.

In 1886 Paul Gauguin (1848-1903) took park in an exhibition of Synthesist painters, he broke away from Impressionism and initiated a style using brilliant colors, attempting meanwhile to create work with a decorative and abstract aspect. He immersed himself in this new approach, rejecting Western civilization and in 1891 he went to Tahiti where he painted many canvases such as this (fig. 246) in which the contrast of color introduces the factor of Variety.

Texture is another factor which helps capture the viewer's attention, it creates variety within the unity and adds to the composition of the subject. Whether there is little texture or a lot

of texture the variety is created through the use of the thickness of the paint. In pictures such as this one on opposite page by Martínez Lozano (called *Texture*) or the extraordinary *14 July* by Van Gogh (figs. 247 & 248 respectively) the variety stems from the thickness of the paint; the *impasto* has the appearance of low relief sculpture.

However, this is not all. In the composition of a landscape the factors already discussed such as unity and variety, the Golden Section, the format, contrasts, textures all come into play, in conjunction with all the norms and factors that determine and accentuate *depth*, the third dimension which we will talk about presently.

244

244 A

243

Fig. 243. John Yardley (b. 1933). *The facade of St Mark's. Venice.* Courtesy of the editorial David & Charles, London. John Yardley is one of the most highly regarded English watercolorists, he has the ability to synthesize forms and colors as you can appreciate in this excellent watercolor painted with black and a few touches of sepia, which brings out the quality of variety to the painting.

Figs. 244 & 244A. Joaquim Mir (1873-1940). *The Port of Tarragona.* Private collection, Barcelona. The variety has been achieved through the bold contrast of colors, by juxtapositioning the complementary colors orange and blue.

Fig. 245. Maurice Prendergast (1859-1924). *St Mark's Square, Venice (a day of sun and showers)*. Private collection. The American watercolorist was fond of brightly colored crowd scenes, these elements provided the element of variety evident here in this watercolor.

Fig. 246. Paul Gauguin (1848-1903). *Tahitian Pastoral*. Hermitage Museum, St. Petersburg. The flat planes of juxtaposed colors create variety with their strong contrasts.

Fig. 247. José Martínez Lozano (b. 1923). *Texture*. Private collection. Martínez Lozano combines this impasto technique with diverse geometrical planes, effectively creating variety and building a strong composition.

Fig. 248. Vincent van Gogh (1853-1890). *Public garden in Arles (the poet's garden)* (detail). Private collection. Van Gogh always used impasto as a factor to create diversity and variety within his pictures.

245

246

248

247

Volume, Contrast and Atmosphere

When you draw or paint you are working in only two dimensions –those of the canvas– height and width. The third dimension, depth, has to be created by you; and basically you do this by representing the contrasts of light and shadow and by the effects of perspective. For example, if you have to draw or paint an egg you start by drawing an oval (fig. 249), up till this point this is nothing more than a flat geometrical shape in two dimensions, height and width. In order to represent an egg you have to represent the third dimension, depth, and this is done by adding the effects of light and shade (fig. 250). Let's suppose that you want to draw or paint a house. You start by drawing the structure of the building seen in perspective (fig. 251). In this line drawing you are representing not only its height and width but also, thanks to perspective you represent the third dimension, depth.

The artist has the following factors to consider when representing depth.

1. **Volume, contrast and atmosphere**
2. **The effect of perspective**
3. **Emphasizing depth using the foreground**
4. **The *coulisse* effect**
5. **Enhancing contrasts**
6. **"Near" and "distant" colors**

As you will see, the representation of depth or the third dimension is one more factor that reveals Unity within Variety. Let me illustrate this.
Velázquez, and all the great masters, offer a classic example by their representation of the third dimension through light and shade i.e. by representing volume and contrast and atmosphere. You can see these effects in figure 252, it is a detail of the famous painting *San Antonio Abad and San Pablo* by Velázquez.
In the next painting (fig. 235), Claude Monet's painting reveals a landscape in which we can appreciate not only volume but also the contrasts of tones and color between the foreground and

the background whose mass of blues creates the impression of the intervening atmosphere. Also note the geometrical structure of the work, a perfect example of Unity within Variety.

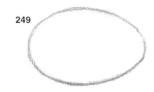

Fig. 249, 250, 251. The line drawing of an egg offers us just two dimensions, height and width (fig. 249). In order to represent the third dimension you have to include the effects of light and shade (fig. 250). In the house seen in perspective, the linear structure is sufficient to represent depth.

Fig. 252. Velázquez (1599-1660). *San Antonio Abad and San Pablo* (detail). Museo del Prado, Madrid.

Fig. 253. Claude Monet (1840-1926). *Cap Martin, near Menton.* Museum of Fine Arts, Boston. Within the diagonal format created by the cliffs.

The Effect of Perspective

254

You only need to look at these breath-taking paintings by Antonio López, Camille Pissarro and Vincent van Gogh (figs. 254, 255 & 256 respectively), to understand that perspective is a basic factor used to represent the third dimension, depth. What's more, in the paintings of Antonio López and Camille Pissarro the atmosphere is almost tangible, represented by the softened colors and haziness in the background. In both paintings there is also a strong geometrical format, look at *Gran Vía, Madrid*, by Antonio López, the immediate foreground the asphalt road painted with traffic signals but the fact that the scene is totally deserted, without cars or people. This creates a dramatic graphic drama, these are two examples of Unity within Variety.

The van Gogh landscape *Field with poppies* (fig. 256) is very different. This is a highly original painting, the aerial viewpoint is evident when you study the perspective, the format minimalizes the sky. This emphasis on parallel perspective reinforces the idea of Unity and on the other hand the diversity of colors in the strips of

255

256

fields give the picture its Variety. It is a different approach, however it is yet another example of skillful composition and interpretation.

Figs. 254, 255 & 256. Antonio López (b. 1936). *Gran Vía*. Private collection. Camille Pissarro (1831-1903). *Le boulevard Montmartre, misty morning 1897*. Private collection, Paris. Vincent van Gogh (1853-1890). *Field with poppies*. Kunsthalle, Bremen. The three paintings are impressive examples of the how depth is created through observation of the effects of perspective.

Emphasizing Depth using the Foreground

This is one of the well tested formulas to represent the third dimension. It consists of altering the viewpoint, trying out a new format. *"The same subject seen from a different angle"* as Cézanne said, so that seen from a little farther back, looked at from one side or the other, you can introduce an eye-catching feature between you and the motif; a tree, a hut, a haystack, etc., you can relate to the object's shape and size and contrast it with the objects situated in the more distant planes of the picture. Imagine for example that you had chosen a mountain village as your subject (fig. 257). In the first viewpoint you have the village as the foreground with the snow capped mountains as a backdrop, however, there is no real sense of depth in the image. Imagine that you take a few steps back, now before you in the immediate foreground you have a tree, figure 258. The sensation of depth becomes far more evident. You can appreciate this same effect in figure 259, a landscape in which I was lucky enough to find a foreground featuring a group of trees on the right and a single tree on the left, a great format for expressing the third dimension.

257

258

259

But what if there is no tree in the foreground?

If that is the case then you should resort to a trick used by the English landscape painters at the end of the 18th century. They would represent the third dimension by painting in some bushes, rocks or undefined margins, scrubbing the paint on giving very little definition —out of focus— as any photographer would say. This approach was justified by Rousseau who said "A spectator viewing a landscape doesn't see what is right at his feet". So, if you do not have any features in the foreground use this trick to help you out. I have used it in this landscape on the outskirts of the city of Cuenca (fig. 260) and I think you'll agree that it has turned out well.

260

Figs. 257 & 258 (photos taken by José M. Parramón). The second photo has been taken from a few meters further back and includes a tree in the foreground which works as a point of reference for the more distant planes, creating an impression of depth for the viewer.

Fig. 259. José M. Parramón (b.1919). *Landscape in Rupit*. Private collection, Barcelona. Here is a well formatted picture, with a group of trees in the foreground on the right and a single tree on the left which create a feeling of depth.

Fig. 260. José M. Parramón (b. 1919). *Villar del Saz*. Private collection. If there are no foreground features to be found, you may decide to paint an undefined, blurred foreground, as I have done in this picture.

The *Coulisse* Effect

The word *coulisse* comes from France where it used to describe the theater set decorations on either side of the stage which allow the actors to enter and exit the scene, what we would call the "wings". The French artists adopted the terminology coulisse to describe a type of composition in which a number of planes in succession created the impression of depth, the third dimension.

You will see examples of this in the following paintings, in the first (fig. 261), the coulisse is created by the two swathes in foreground and the group of houses in the middle ground, by the backdrop of the nearest mountain and the mountains behind in the distance (look at the diagram, fig. 261A). In the next image, apart from the impression of depth created by the river in the foreground the *coulisse* is created by the groups of houses which reach back in successive planes (fig. 262 & 262A).

261

261 A

Figs. 262 & 262A. Joaquim Mir (1873-1940). *Bridge in Les Escaldes. Andorra*. Pujadas collection. Another clear example of how the arrangement of successive planes creates depth, emphasized by the contrast of the river in the foreground with the dramatic scene set against the light, adeptly expressed by Joaquim Mir.

262

262 A

Figs. 261 & 261A. José M. Parramón (b. 1919). *Mountain landscape*. Private collection. I painted this landscape with the coulisse effect in mind, the impression of depth is created by superimposing successive planes.

Enhancing Contrasts

We have already discussed contrast and atmosphere as two of the factors employed by an artist to represent depth. Let me just remind you of two key rules regarding contrast and atmosphere that any artist should bear in mind when painting a landscape:

1. The foreground should always be brighter and more contrasted than the more distant planes.
2. In order to distance the further planes, soften the colors in the distance which have a tendency towards blues, purples and grays.

It is worth repeating these two rules yet again, despite the fact I have mentioned them so often in my books, and now consider the advice of Leonardo da Vinci who stated in his book *The Treatise on Painting*, *"If you give a detailed finish to objects in the distance they will seem closer and not further away"*.

In order to reiterate this important rule have a look at the adjacent watercolor by the English artist Edward Seago (fig. 263) who provides us with a clear example of how to interpret the contrasts and atmosphere in order to represent depth, the third dimension. Now let's consider how to enhance these contrasts, or in other words to introduce contrasts when they do not exist in the subject, also following the advice of Leonardo when he said:

"The background framing an object can be shaded in the parts where the object is lit and brightened in the areas where the object is in shadow".
Every artist of every generation has used this trick which I call "enhanced contrasts" to good effect. It is a system which defines the outlines of objects, distinguishes different objects and makes the individual shapes stand out. If you look at figure 264, you will

see how Cézanne painted contrast that did not exist in reality, to highlight and define forms and their outlines. I think that this is yet another way of representing the third dimension.

Fig. 263. Edward Seago (1910-1974). *The stone quay, Ponza.* **Courtesy of the editorial David & Charles. London. Seago gives us a perfect example of clarity and strength of colors in the foreground contrasted by the fading colors and unfocused definition in the background, following the advice of Leonardo da Vinci of** *"distancing the objects* **that are further away."**

263

264

Figs. 264 and 264A. Paul Cézanne (1839-1906). *The bridge at Mennecy.* **Musée d'Orsay, Paris. "Enhancing contrasts" is effectively painting with colors that are darker or lighter than those that exist in the original model, in order to highlight and distinguish certain shapes. Look in the diagram below (fig. 264A) which indicates certain points in the painting where Cézanne has enhanced the contrasts.**

264A

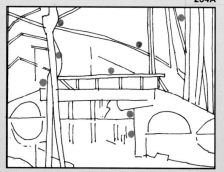

Near and Distant Colors

If you paint a layer of yellow and add a strip of orange above, then continue with a strip of red above which you put a strip of green, blue, etc., finishing off with a light bluish gray (fig. 265), you will notice that the yellow and the orange appear "closer" whereas the blues "recede", and the reds and greens appear to stay in the middle ground. This concept of near and distant colors was discussed and put into practice by the Dutch and Flemish landscape painters of the sixteenth and seventeenth centuries as you would have seen in this book from page 18 onwards.

But in practice it can prove difficult, if not impossible to find this arrangement of brilliant colors in the same order as the range of colors in figure 265. However, it is just a question of approximations, as in the watercolor below (fig. 266), by altering, adding, and brightening colors in comparison to the original landscape (fig. 267), developing and interpreting this spectrum of near and distant colors to enhance the impression of depth and following Plato's principal of Unity within Variety.

So, without more ado let's prepare to move on into another world –a complex world– a world of change, of imagination, of exaggeration: on the following page we will talk of *interpretation*.

265

266

Fig. 265. You can clearly see that yellow is a near color and blue is a distant color.

Fig. 266 & 267. In the studio, Jordi Segú has attempted to use the concept of near and distant colors to his advantage, he has intensified the yellows, greens and blues present in the original.

267

The Process of Interpreting a Landscape

Interpretation depends greatly on your imagination. By interpreting the subject you are changing it and your imagination intervenes to alter the reality. Look up the word imagination in a dictionary and it is defined as follows:

A. The ability to form mental images
B. The ability to combine images

So, in order to interpret, the artist has to be able to picture a series of images and to combine this series with what he sees in front of him. In this case it is a landscape which he modifies, alters and develops to create his own image. It is useful to recall the belief of many great artists regarding the importance of painting a picture from what you see "within your head". *"Painters who copy a subject will never communicate a lively sense of Nature"* (Delacroix).
"We see Nature as something ordinary, the artist has to see it and paint it as something fantastic and fabulous" (Chagall). *"The painter has to let his impressions and his personal vision take shape in his paintings"* (Picasso).
Let me develop a few ideas along the lines of these thoughts, on the artist's processes of imagination and fantasy, as well as some rules and regulations about artistic interpretation.
The first step, as always, consists of studying the subject for a considerable length of time, analyzing its artistic possibilities, establishing if there is a geometric format and if it can be improved upon by changing a few details. You also have to analyze each element of the whole and decide if you want to suppress certain details such as posts or fences, walls, even houses. Naturally, in the course of this imaginative analysis the artist also considers the contrasts in the foreground, the effects of the atmosphere on the most distant planes, the general range of colours... At this point, when the artist starts to imagine the alterations of shapes,

colors, contrasts of tone or color etc. they refer to their picture library, "a mental archive of images and visual memories" which we all carry in our heads. The artist may remember or imagine the picture called *The reapers* by Van Gogh, with its yellow sky and bluish background (fig. 268), and imagine applying these same colors to the sky and the background of their landscape. Or maybe he remembers a landscape by Manet, *Le pavé de Chailly* in which the sky is a very light cream color and the trees blend with the background in a blur of warm dull color (fig. 269), and he imagines the same background in the landscape that they are looking at. And they also bring to mind the contrast of that

farmhouse in the foreground which they saw only a few days ago drenched in sunlight and surrounded by rich deep greens (fig. 270), they imagine applying this same contrast to the scene that they now how in front of them, etc. (consider figs 271 & 272).
This ability to imagine and see other colors, other contrasts, to "see" a different landscape to that which is ahead of you, means that reality has to give way to the colors and the landscape which the artist sees in his imagination. The artist combines what he sees ahead of him with his imagination and memories, working his way mentally across the landscape considering possibilities, enhancing accentuating, suppressing (figs. 273

268

270

269

271

272

Fig. 268. Van Gogh (1853-1890). *The reapers.* Rodin Museum, Paris.

Fig. 269. Claude Monet (1840-1926). *Le pavé de Chailly*, Musée d'Orsay, Paris.

Fig. 270. *The house at Hostalets.* Photo by José M. Parramón.

and 274), entering into the land of creativity which I believe can be defined as a *new outlook when faced with something that we want to change*. In other words, an active attitude towards the work distinguishing it from reality and from a representation of the past, and which can result in something that you have never seen or imagined before.

Some guidelines about the art of interpretation.

However you have interpreted what I have said so far, there are three verbs that clearly summarize the art of interpreting a landscape:

Enlarge, Reduce, Suppress

Enlarge, highlight, exaggerate, intensify this or that color, the contrasts in the foreground, the size of this tree, of that house, and intensify the color of the sky.

Reduce, fade, soften, reduce the size of the trees, the width of the road, the color of the haystack, the height of the mountains, the contrasts in the middle ground, the volume of the clouds.

Suppress, eliminate, hide, ignore the telegraph pole, the car in the background, the modern house, the asphalt road, the weeds in the foreground, the tractor and the lorry, etc.

273

Fig. 271 (opposite page, right). Guillem Fresquet. *Landscape.* Private collection.

Fig. 272. (opposite page, below). *The inlet in Bilbao.* Private collection.

Fig. 273. José M. Parramón (b.1919). *Fishermen's quay,* Barcelona. Private collection. (Photo José M. Parramón). The landscape is the same but interpretation has altered the appearance which I imagined from a higher viewpoint, the cold colors of the original have been altered to the warm colors you see in the painting.

274

The Subject: Enemy Number One

At the beginning of the twentieth century, the writer Léo Larguier published an account of Cézanne's ideas and thoughts passed on to him by Cézanne's son Lucien. The master of Aix was said to have believed that:

"Painting is not about slavishly copying the model, but more about capturing a harmony between many different related factors which must be processed by developing your own vision, interpreting it as a new and original concept".

Everything that you paint and that you want to interpret with a contemporary attitude will be in line with Cézanne's beliefs. We all strive to paint reinventing the subject as a "new and original concept", we all believe that *"painting is not about slavishly copying the model"*. You and I believe this and subscribe to Cézanne's advice to the letter, but, in practice it is another story.
Listen to what the famous Post-Impressionist Pierre Bonnard has to say on the subject in an interview with the journalist Angele Lamotte in 1943:

"I tried to paint them –the roses– directly, with precision, but I became carried away with the details... I found I was sinking, that I wasn't getting anywhere. I had lost the first impression, I couldn't recall my first impulse, the vision which dazzled me, my starting point".

The presence of the model or subject is an obstacle to a painter while they are painting.

Delacroix expressed the same idea when he said *"The model absorbs everything, leaving nothing for the painter"*.
Bonnard continued by saying:

"The starting point is always an idea; having the subject before you
as you work is a temptation, the artist runs the risk of letting the direct vision take over, forgetting his first impulse... and he ends up giving in to chance, setting down each shadow he sees and capturing details that never interested him in the first place".**

In this interview with Angele Lamotte, Bonnard also talked about

275

276

Figs. 275, 276 & 277. I was in Venice and as well as painting two pictures I took various photos, one of them was of the Grand Canal (fig. 276). Remembering that Claude Monet painted this same subject I searched in my books when I got home and, sure enough, found that Monet painted two versions of *The Grand Canal in Venice*, one in the Museum of Fine Arts, San Francisco (fig. 275) and the other in the Museum of Fine Arts in Boston (fig. 278). Two versions which are both exceptional demonstrations of his capacity for imagination.

in the Art of Interpretation

Monet's fears of being overwhelmed by the subject. He said:

"Claude Monet would paint before the subject but only for about ten minutes. He didn't give things (the model) time to take possession of him".

Perhaps it wasn't ten minutes, perhaps he would paint for fifteen or even twenty, but the fact is that this comment coincides with the fact that Monet, as you know, would work on various canvases at once (up to nine at a time) and it is also certain that he would retouch and finish his paintings in the studio (figs. 275 & 278).

The subject has a charm, as alluring as a mermaid's song, how does one avoid being seduced? Bonnard provides us with an answer.

"Do what Cézanne did, Cézanne had a firm idea of what he wanted to achieve when he was before the subject, and he only took from Nature that which fitted with this idea... things... only if they appeared as in his imagination."

John Berger, the English critic and painter, wrote in his book *The Look*

Fig. 277. Paul Cézanne (1839-1906). *Mountain Sainte-Victoire.* **Collection of Mr. and Mrs. Carroll S. Tyson, Philadelphia.This is one of the last painting of the series of fifty five that Cézanne painted of Mountain Sainte-Victoire, when the artist put into practice his theory that he** *"only took from Nature that which fitted with his ideas",* **one of the notions that were to prelude cubism.**

277

278

of Things "The greatest heroism of Cézanne's self discipline consisted of his capacity to observe the picture he was painting with the same attention and objectivity with which he studied the subject. How easy it sounds. As easy as walking on water".

One can imagine Cézanne in front of the subject, before one of his landscapes (fig. 277) *"He would look with intense concentration at the subject for minutes on end (those who had the opportunity to see him paint described this) and suddenly he would turn his head towards the canvas and add a single dash of color, one single brushstroke. Attempting to shape his idea, his own conception of the landscape, muttering to himself over and over 'As I see it...as I see it.' ".*

Fig. 279. José M. Parramón (b. 1919). *Carboneras* (Cuenca,
Spain). Private collection. I was on a walking and painting trip,
one August in the province of Cuenca and I was going to have
lunch after finishing a painting, when I saw these cumulus
clouds and this village surrounded by brown earth... It was two
in the afternoon, I was hungry and tired. But the clouds, the
colors... I stopped the car, set up my easel and painted on one
of the canvases I had in the trunk, a number 10 landscape.
I started with the clouds. I finished just after 6 o'clock. "Paris
well deserves a Mass," said Henry IV when he forswore
Protestantism to be the King of France. And these clouds, this
land and these colors, despite my hunger and my exhaustion,
well deserved a picture.

INCIDENTAL DETAILS: THE SKY, CLOUDS, EARTH, TREES, SHADOWS, THE SEA AND FIGURES IN LANDSCAPE PAINTINGS

Now we are entering into the realm of details that appear in any landscape, we will be studying the colors of the sky when it is clear, half overcast and cloudy; the colors of the earth when lit by the sun or when in shadow, earth roads and ploughed fields; the structure of trees, their trunks, crowns and foliage, seen close-up and from afar; and the color of shadows, an aspect applicable to each detail of landscape painting. We will also cast a look at the sea, rocks, beaches and boats, finishing up with a brief study of figure representation in landscape. All this and more with graphic examples, explanations and diagrams painted both in oils and watercolor.
Turn over right away to find out more.

The Sky and Clouds

From the era of the Dutch artists (who were featured on pages 20 to 23) until Monet and the Impressionists, and continuing until Fortuny and contemporary artists such as Seago, landscape scenes with predominant cloudy skies have always been a subject that the artists have found rewarding to paint (figs. 280, 281, & 282).

The English painter John Constable also painted a great number of cloud studies both in watercolor and in oils. The one that you can see on the opposite page (fig. 283) is a study in watercolor painted in Suffolk by Constable. It is dated 15th September 1830 in his writing on the back. Constable always wrote the place and date when he painted studies like this. Constable believed that the sky is a seminal part of landscape. He wrote *"The sky is a fundamental element, the light source which governs the entire landscape"*.

The impressionist, Alfred Sisley also considered that the sky has as a very important role to play in landscape painting: *"The sky is not simply a background wash, an abyss of brightness. The sky is brother to the planes and is itself composed of planes just as the earth is. I always start*

280

280 A

282

281

Figs. 280 & 280A. Claude Monet (1840-1926). *The Seine at Argenteuil.* Musée d'Orsay, Paris. A cloud painting, the clouds are the main focus of the landscape here, they also emphasize the geometric format of the painting, strong contrasts enrich the artistic composition.

Fig. 281. Mariano Fortuny (1834-1874). *Landscape.* Museo del Prado, Madrid. A complex skyscape for a watercolor, Fortuny had to carefully save the white spaces for the clouds, not only filling in the blue of the sky around each cloud but also fading the blue towards the horizon, another difficult task.

Fig. 282. Edward Seago (1910-1974. *The fence around the marshes.* Courtesy of the editorial David & Charles, London. This skyscape is a result of a number of watercolor washes, the first layers have been painted using wet on wet and on top of these a number of layers have been painted on dry, or with a half dry pencil, (the paint applied with a rubbing action). This sky is a lesson in technique.

Fig. 283 (opposite page, above). John Constable (1776-1837). *Cloud study.* Victoria and Albert Museum, London. For Constable, the skies were an important and attractive motif to study. Constable made a large number of sketches of clouds in both watercolor and oils.

283

with the sky". I do too, and so, for that matter do the majority of artists. This is because when you paint clouds you have to catch them quickly before they alter and because the professional painter feels the need to "fill the gaps". This means eliminating the white spaces on the canvas to avoid the negative effects caused by the Law of Simultaneous Contrasts, a law which says:

A color becomes lighter or darker dependant on the color which surrounds it (figs. 284 & 285).

See how this optical effect works in the examples on the right, considering that because of the law of simultaneous contrasts, the white of the cloud surrounded by deep blue sky (fig. 284) seems whiter than the same white cloud in a lighter blue sky (fig. 285). We will talk about this rule again when we reach the practical exercises for landscape painting.

For the time being, I suggest that you practice drawing skies, copying them from a photo or another illustration. You will need chalks or pastels in ultramarine blue, white and black, a blue sheet of Canson mid-tint paper, something delicate to blur and smudge the colors (you can always use your fingers), and a soft eraser. I made this study with these same materials (figs. 286 & 287). I recommend that you also try it, besides being enjoyable, it is a good exercise.

Figs. 284 & 285. As you can appreciate, because of the law of simultaneous contrasts the white of the cloud on the deep blue background (fig. 284) stands out whiter than the same cloud on a paler background.

Figs. 286 & 287. I have created this sky, on Canson mid-tint paper tinted Ultramarine blue, using a stick of hard white *Koh-i-noor* chalk, and black chalk for the mountains.

284   **285**

286   **287**

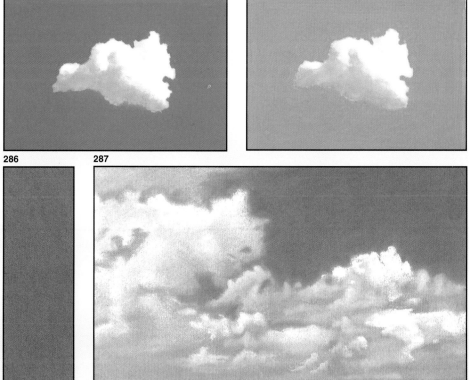

Clear Skies, Cloudy Skies

288

288A

Let's set color in the skies. We will start with clear skies, bearing in mind that they are more intensely blue as you look up, painted with a touch more ultramarine blue and a hint of carmine and it is slightly lighter as the sky comes down to meet with the horizon, occasionally with the slightest tendency towards yellowish cream. Study figure 288A which illustrates these general characteristics, with the colors used to paint a clear blue sky (fig. 288).

So, as you know the sky is rarely blue, even a clear sky or practically clear sky can be gray, orange, pink etc. but it always has a tendency towards a more intense color higher up, further from the horizon (figs. 289 & 290), except at sunrise or sunset when, whether or not the sun is visible, it illuminates the horizon, intensifying the colors (figs. 291 & 292).

These characteristics of clear skies –more color higher up and less color towards the horizon– are the same for half overcast skies or cloudy skies, given that the cloud cover is nothing more than a backdrop studded with clouds with their highlights and shadows.

And now we are going to paint cloudy skies, starting with a storm cloud filled sky. Storm clouds often take up unusual shapes, the sky is a combination of stratus and cumulus clouds (cumulostratus) with a tendency towards darker colors higher in the sky with a combination of mid gray and dark gray. Look at figures 293 & 294 which are an example of this. When painting with oils, we still need to consider how a sky full of cumulus clouds is developed both in watercolor and in oils. You will see this process explained step by step on the following pages, with brief explanations about the techniques to be used with both media.

289

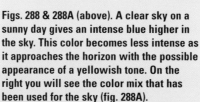

290

Figs. 288 & 288A (above). A clear sky on a sunny day gives an intense blue higher in the sky. This color becomes less intense as it approaches the horizon with the possible appearance of a yellowish tone. On the right you will see the color mix that has been used for the sky (fig. 288A).

Figs. 289 & 290. The sky is rarely blue; it can be gray, pink, cream, etc.

Figs. 291 & 292 (opposite page, above). I painted this sunset in watercolor, of the Atlantic Ocean in Galicia, Northern Spain.

A simple sketch captures the amazing chromatic range of a sunset.

Figs. 293 & 294 (opposite page, below). A cloudy stormy sky, the huge dark gray clouds above are contrasted with the white cumulus and stratus clouds, with chunks of blue sky showing through. A delightful subject to paint in oils, and a good exercise in skyscape painting.

291

292

294

293

Painting Skies in Watercolor and Oils

I would not be exaggerating if I said that to paint a skyscape with clouds –either in watercolor or oils– is one of the hardest exercises for any student of art. There are two basic reasons for this; clouds are constantly on the move and

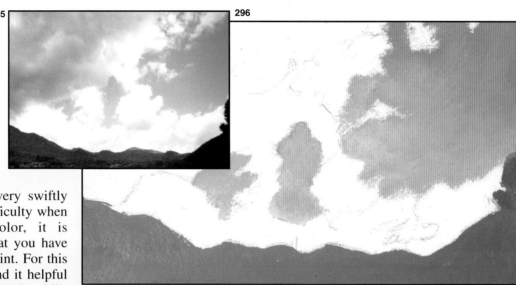

so you have to work very swiftly and, with the added difficulty when painting with watercolor, it is impossible to undo what you have done, to regret and repaint. For this very reason you will find it helpful to study skyscapes painted by skilled watercolorists, demonstrating how important it is to start with a sketch –top speed, make it snappy!– of the outlines of the clouds, keeping in mind that layers of superimposed color are not a feature of a good watercolor, the blue of the sky, deeper at the top, lighter towards the horizon, should be described with a single definitive wash, with white spaces reserved for the clouds. Don't even consider reinforcing the color or applying a second coat of blue, the effort will be useless!

Painting in oils is less complicated because of the fact that oil paints allow you to paint light colors over dark colors and to overpaint and rectify mistakes. You can even start painting the backdrop of the skyscape blue without defining the contours or outlines of the clouds.

Let us look at these ideas in practice, a skyscape in oils (figs. 295 to 298) and another in watercolor (figs. 299 to 302).

Painting in oils

Fig. 295. The subject, a storm cloud at the top contrasted by a clear patch nearer the horizon on the right.

Fig. 296. A few simple lines describe the cloud formation and then I start to paint the sky, a more intense blue at the top with spaces left

300

299

301

302

unpainted for the clouds. I also paint in the mountain range.

Fig. 297. I describe the dark stain of the storm cloud in the top left with ultramarine blue, Van Dyck brown and white. I add a strip of green in the foreground, a tree on the right and I sketch in a little house and some trees on the left.

Fig. 298. I make the gray of the storm cloud more intense and add to the blue of the sky and give volume to the cumulus clouds with a mixture of ultramarine blue, Van Dyck brown and a touch of ochre.

Painting in watercolor
Fig. 299. The landscape is a flat plain, the sky has cumulus clouds that seem as if they are turning into stratus clouds.
Fig. 300. First I try to describe the plain in fairly neutral tones. Next, I draw in the outline of the cloud formations in pencil.
Fig. 301. With one single wash of paint I add the blue of the sky, reserving the white spaces for the clouds and wetting and drawing off the paint to extend the faint traces of cloud across the sky.
Fig. 302. Now the clouds must be shaped with blues and grays –cobalt blue, a touch of carmine and a hint of brown (not so much that you would notice, the paint color is blue)– combined with water for the wash. I add some finishing touches to the details in the foreground and its finished.

Earth Colors

303

304

The earth tones and colors found in fields, roads and mountains vary greatly depending on the type of soil, the distance, the season and the weather conditions. They do have, however, some aspects in common; generally the color of the earth is darker when it is cultivated, lighter in untended land and even lighter on dirt roads or tracks. The weather conditions, damp, rainy or dry, will change and darken the color of the ground, and viewing at long distance will alter and fade colors to grays and blues.

This variety of color is evident when you compare cultivated ground with a dirt road or path. Any ploughed land, worked by hand or by tractor, is made up of peaks and troughs which create shadows, deepening the color, the ground will become even darker if irrigated or rained on. By contrast, dirt roads or paths are worn smooth, they absorb water better and dry more quickly so they show less variation of color. The shadows cast over uneven ploughed land are dark, their color dominated by Sienna, red carmine and blue. The shadows cast on the road are bluer. Compare these tones and variations of color on the following page (figs. 305 & 306).

Carefully consider these colors, bearing in mind that earth colors are never uniform. Try to see and capture the variety of shades and tones resulting from the reflections and variations in color caused by the uneven surface, the effect of the light, etc. Whether it has a dark or light base color, little patches and hints of different colors should be introduced along with or on top of the base color, touches of color which give variety to the general appearance. Have a look at figures 303 & 304 to see how Camille Pissarro painted the color of the dirt road; weaving a combination of colors, introducing hints and touches of other colors into his landscape *Going into the village*. Note the direction of the brushstrokes which is generally horizontal, particularly when depicting roads and paths. Don't be impatient and don't improvise. Interpret, but keep your original subject and its colors in mind.

305

306

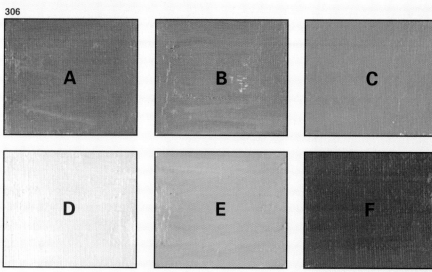

Figs. 303 & 304 (opposite page). Camille Pissarro (1831-1903). *Going into the village*. Musée d'Orsay, Paris. The rich variety in the hints of color that Pissarro used to describe the road and the green patches either side can be clearly seen in these pictures, especially in the enlarged detail below.

Figs. 305 & 306. The color of the earth is made up of many different hints of color, dependant upon whether it is uncultivated or ploughed, in the sun or in the shade. You can see these differences in this painting and in the swatches of color in figure 306.

The Color of Shadows

307

Fig. 307. This is the landscape that I am going to paint to study the colors of the shadows.

Fig. 308 (below). Notice in this image the amont of blue that exits in the landscape taking into account that the greens and other colors of the shadows are made up basically with the color blue.

In the history of art there is a "before" and an "after" when discussing the color of shadows. The earlier period is dominated by painters such as Giotto, Leonardo, Rafael, Titian, Caravaggio, etc. who painted shadows which would darken the color of the immediate area, generally by applying a color called bitumen, a sort of deep brownish color which was used until the middle of the nineteenth century. And then there is the "after" period whose key protagonists were the Impressionists who revolutionised art theories; language, style and color. Most importantly they revolutionised light, they painted outdoors and discovered the color blue in shadows, *I am searching constantly for blue* said Van Gogh. The arrival of Impressionism coincided with the discoveries by the French chemist M. Chévreul about complementary colors which are linked to the color of shadows. Because of the progression in understanding and study of shadows we now have a clearer understanding of the correct colors to use for painting shadows:

The color blue is always present in any shadow

mix blue with a deeper version of the original color

mix the resulting color with the complementary color of each particular original color

Let us consider this and try it out. I am going to paint a landscape (fig. 307), first just using shades of blue (fig. 308). I will then paint the same landscape but this time resolving the tonality of the shadows with a darker tone of the original color, for example, the tree is a yellow green color so I paint the areas in shadow with a darker green, emerald green mixed with dark brown such as raw umber (fig. 309). Next I paint a third version, adding to the shadowed

308

309

310

area of each object the color that is complementary to the original color of the object. (fig. 310). Finally I paint the same subject once more, only this time I describe the shadows by using a mix of the three colors already mentioned; blue, a deeper version of the original color and the complementary color to the original color (fig. 311).

This formula that I have explained and demonstrated with this landscape can interpret the subject in a number of ways depending on how you resolve the shadows and the style of painting; tonally, in an Impressionist, Post-Impressionist, Fauvist or Expressionist style.

311

Fig. 309 (opposite page). The same landscape painted using a darker version of the original color to describe the effect of shadow on that color.

Fig. 310 (above). Here I have used the complementary color of the original color to paint the areas in shadow; a reddish orange in the shadow of the houses, a carmine in the shadow of the green, etc.

Fig. 311. And this is the final result. The color of the shadows is the consequence of mixing blue, the original color of the object and the complementary color of the original color.

Trees

Once again I am going to use another quote, Ingres commented on the importance of drawing, *"You only paint as well as you draw"*, reminding one that skies, clouds and trees are painted as they are drawn. Put another way, *good painting depends on good drawing*.

It comes as no surprise therefore, that the majority of artists, all the great masters both past and contemporary have filled blocks of drawing paper with landscape sketches, studies of trees in particular.

Talking of drawing blocks, I have a book on Léonard Saint-Michel from the Carnets de Dessin collection (Henri Crépel Publishing) and under the title of *Corot's Universe* there are 31 reproductions of Corot drawings and sketches, eight of which are figure studies, ten are drawings or sketches of landscapes featuring large trees in the foreground and thirteen are tree studies (fig. 314). So out of the 31 Corot drawings, 23 are of trees.

Van Gogh also showed this preference for studying trees (figs. 312 & 313) and much earlier, in 1820, Constable did this magnificent study of fir trees drawn with a lead pencil (fig. 315, following page). Finally, have a look at the study of a tree trunk done in lead pencil on light gray paper by the American artist, Asher B. Durand (1796-1886) and the study that I did of an olive tree, also using lead pencil (figs. 316 & 317).

All you need is a sketching block of A4 size (21 cm x 30 cm) and a lead B6 pencil or a carbon pencil and all you have to do in order to imitate these famous artists is go out into the countryside and make sketches of trees. It is a very interesting exercise and whatsmore it is crucial if you want to paint trees well, so that you can paint good landscapes.

312

313

314

Figs. 312 & 313. Vincent van Gogh (1853-1890). *Roots of a tree on sandy soil.* **Rijksmuseum Kröller-Muller, Otterlo.** *The apricot tree in flower.* **Rijksmuseum, Amsterdam. Van Gogh drew and painted trees on many occasions and using a variety of media, in these examples he was working with pencil, chalk, ink and watercolor (fig. 312), and black chalk, and watercolor on Whatman paper.**

Fig. 314. Jean-Baptiste Camille Corot (1796-1875). *Tree study.* **Musée du Louvre, Paris. Many tree studies by Corot survive, they were drawn from nature usually with a lead pencil, in this case on colored paper.**

315

316

317

Fig. 315. John Constable (1776-1837).
Fir trees in Hampstead. Victoria &
Albert Museum, London. A superb
study drawn from nature using a
lead pencil.

Fig. 316. Asher B. Durand (1796-1886).
Life studies. Metropolitan Museum
of Art, New York. An American
engraver and painter, Durand's
landscapes were inspired by the
Dutch sixteenth century artists,
Hobbema in particular.

Fig. 317. José M. Parramón (b. 1919).
Nature study. Drawing in lead pencil
2B and 6B.

How to Paint Trees

You are already aware that to paint a landscape in oils it is of primary importance to know how to draw while painting, that means to draw with the paintbrush. Cézanne explained it thus: **"When you paint, you draw. The precision of the drawing creates the modelling and color simultaneously".**

This ability to draw with the paintbrush is vital to painting trees. Painting in oils does give you some advantages; you can start by drawing the landscape and trees with charcoal, adding light and shadows and fixing it before painting over the sketch, which is very convenient. Also bear in mind that oils are opaque, you can always alter and repaint with light colors over dark. When oil painting it is perfectly normal to paint the lighter areas over dark colors, when introducing patches of light between tree branches for example (fig. 318). These tactics are not possible when painting with watercolors; watercolor is not opaque, it doesn't cover as oils do and it is impossible to paint over a sketch with shadows already added as the lines would be visible through the transparent watercolor paint. In addition there is the complication of masking white spaces, the bright patches or points of light, the dots of light visible through leafy branches for example (fig. 319).

Another point to consider is that when painting landscapes in oils or watercolor, apart from creating a well constructed image you must study and express the factor of synthesis. This is achieved by drawing or paint-ing using the minimum number of lines, looking at the model through half closed eyes in order to eliminate the excess details (fig. 320) and painting with a thick paintbrush, this is so that you avoid giving in to the temptation of including each little detail which could convert the painting into an academic study like the Dutch who painted the trees in their landscapes leaf by leaf. Synthesis is important in each and every part of the landscape including the trees. A synthesis which, in this case, is maximised when describing trees in the background (figs. 321 & 321A). Trees in the middle ground and foreground can be depicted with blocks or planes of color (fig. 322) or by representing the masses of leaves with a series of brushstrokes or using *impasto*, as Cézanne or Van Gogh did (figs. 323 & 324), or with little comma–like dabs of paint, as Monet did (fig. 325).

Fig. 318. Camille Pissarro (1831-1903). *Going into the village* (detail). **Musée d'Orsay, Paris. The oil paint is opaque and Pissarro demonstrates this when he paints touches of blue amongst the branches where the sky shows through.**

318

319

320

Fig. 319. In this watercolor study of a tree I have had to reserve the patches of light from the start, painting around the white spaces between the leaves to give the impression of the sky showing through.

Fig. 320. Looking at the subject through half closed eyes is a technique that makes it easier to see the subject in synthesis, your vision is restricted to seeing the large masses without seeing too much detail.

321

321 A

322

323

324

325

Fig. 321 & 321A (above). When a subject such as this tree is in the background, use synthesis to abbreviate the details to simple blocks of color.

Fig. 322 (above, right). José M. Parramón (b. 1919). *Landscape with trees*. Private collection, Barcelona. These trees in the foreground have been painted with synthesis, the individual leaves are not detailed but summarised by representing the volume and mass of the leaves.

Fig. 323. Paul Cézanne. *Trees in a park*. Pushkin Museum, Moscow. Cézanne painted these trees using patches of diagonal brushstrokes, synthesising the mass of the leaves.

Fig. 324. Vincent van Gogh (1853-1890). *The rocks* (detail). Museum of Fine Arts, Boston. Van Gogh described the trees in this landscape using impasto of thick paint applied so each stroke is visible.

Fig. 325. Claude Monet (1840-1926). *Field with poplars* (detail). Courtesy of the Museum of Fine Arts, Boston. The delicate brushstrokes and the application of light colors on top of a darker background describes the shape and color of the trees.

Ballestar Paints a Tree in Watercolor, Step by Step

Here we have a tree painted in watercolor. My colleague Vicenç Ballestar is going to take us through a practical exercise; a step by step discovery of the complications inherent in watercolor in comparison to oil painting. I recommend that you follow him to the letter, carefully studying the pictures and accompanying text (figs. 326-332).

Figs. 326 & 327. Ballestar draws and paints with his left hand. He begins the charcoal sketch of the tree that you can see in figure 326, first he draws the tree and the strip of land in the foreground, he starts by drawing in the trunk and a few branches, then adding the masses of leaves, capturing the outline in a rapid line drawing. He is working on Fabriano paper 55 cm x 33 cm (fig. 327).

327

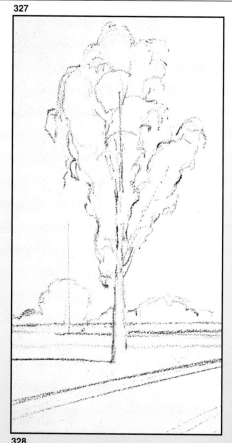

326

Fig. 328. Next Ballestar wets the top section of the paper, the sky, with a 4 cm paintbrush. He waits until the paper is a little drier and he paints the sky omitting the tree, adding color to the background; blue towards the horizon, softening the color higher up. He then turns to the strip of land, painting it with a wash of ochre and raw Sienna and a little olive green. He strengthens the color of the sky at the top and then adds some trees in the background with olive green and permanent green which he then darkens with Hooker green and cobalt blue. The tarmac road is painted with diagonal brushstrokes with a mixture of Van Dyck brown and ultramarine blue. He then starts to paint the tree beginning with the trunk which he starts with ochre and vermilion, he then moves to the highlights in the crown of the tree, using ochre and Hooker green and reserving white spaces –the gaps between the leaves where the sky shows through. He starts to add the interplay of light and shade adding Hooker green and ultramarine blue to the parts in shadow, painting some patches on wet so that the light and dark tones merge together.

328

329

Fig. 329. Now he takes up a number 6 sable brush to detail the crown of the tree, describing it a brushstroke at a time, applying dark colors over lighter colors as if he were drawing with the paintbrush, describing each leaf, the result is an effective synthesis of color, the interplay of light and shade is captured in the mix of darker green over the lighter green. He paints the branches of the eucalyptus with ochre and vermilion using a number 4 brush.

Fig. 330. Talking of brushes, have a look at this photo of the selection of brushes that Ballestar regularly uses to paint watercolor and that he has used to paint this tree. Three synthetic brushes 1 cm, 2 cm and 4 cm wide and three round sable brushes number 4, number 6 and number 12.

Figs. 331 & 332. Let us see how Ballestar finishes the tree, working on the foliage from top to bottom with this same technique, adding the shadow cast by the tree on the strip of land, lifting off a white space to add the pole in the background, using a 1 cm brush on its side, wetting the area and absorbing the color (fig. 331). He keeps adding finishing touches to the tree, introducing some darker touches and strengthening the color of the trunk and the branches (fig. 332). Finally he works on the colors and details of the background, the trees and the white wall on the right, fence posts on the left. For the color of the tarmac in the foreground he adds a shadow in ultramarine blue carmine and Van Dyck brown. Then he signs it.

330

332

331

Water, Rivers and Boats

In August 1869, five years before the first Impressionist exhibition (which took place on 15 April 1874), Claude Monet wrote to his friend Bazille. *"I have a vision, a painting for which I have already made some unsatisfactory sketches, but it is still only a dream, to paint the bathing spot at Grenouillère. Renoir is also going to paint this scene"* (fig. 333).

La Grenouillère was a resort on the outskirts of Paris and Monet's "dream" to paint a picture of that jetty with boats, swimmers, trees, the water and its reflections, was a vision of the first impressionist painting. There was no specific theme composed in the studio, just an everyday scene; it was not a large canvas, it measures 75 cm x 100 cm; the theme was contemporary and the painting was filled with bright light and rapid brushstrokes full of contrasts and colors. This painting was a radical departure, the glistening water was the central motif which captured the viewer's attention. Monet and Renoir and all the impressionists painted the water and the reflections of the river Seine and the sea. They also painted the reflections of buildings in water as Monet did when painting the waters of the Thames in London (fig. 334). Renoir and Monet, along with other impressionists also studied boats; moored sailing boats on the beach and in port or at sea (fig. 335). This is *marine painting* or *seascape*, a classic subject which has much in common with landscape painting and

offers a host of artistic possibilities. Technically speaking, marine paintings can present a number of difficulties related to perspective; drawing boats in perspective and the correct perspective of reflections.

Drawing or painting large or small boats is simply a problem of understanding their structure, dimensions and proportions, calculating the width of the boat in relation to its length and height. This issue can be resolved by making a preliminary sketch drawn in perspective (fig. 336). Which makes the drawing or painting of the boat easier.

The problem of perspective with reflected images can be summed up by the concept that the image reflected in the waters of a river or on the sea is an inverse duplicate of the object, i.e. you have to exactly repeat the drawing or painting of that object but upside down, using the same perspective, the same vanishing

points and the same horizon line. This is illustrated by the sketch painted on the quay in Barcelona (fig. 337).

If you are lucky enough to live near or travel to a port, river or lake, take advantage of this and paint the water, the boats, the reflections, the port or beach, the sea... I am going to explain how on the following page.

Fig. 333. Claude Monet, *La Grenouillère*, **Metropolitan Museum of Art, New York. Monet's painting was a breakthrough, he initiated the impressionist style here, for the first time a picture featuring figures, painted from nature, on a small canvas painted rapidly capturing contrasts and brilliant colors.**

Fig. 334. Claude Monet. *The Houses of Parliament*, **London. Musée d'Orsay, Paris. During his stay in London, Monet painted a number of similar images of the Thames wrapped in a mysterious cloak of mist which Monet captured through the synthesis of the forms and colors and the golden reflections.**

333

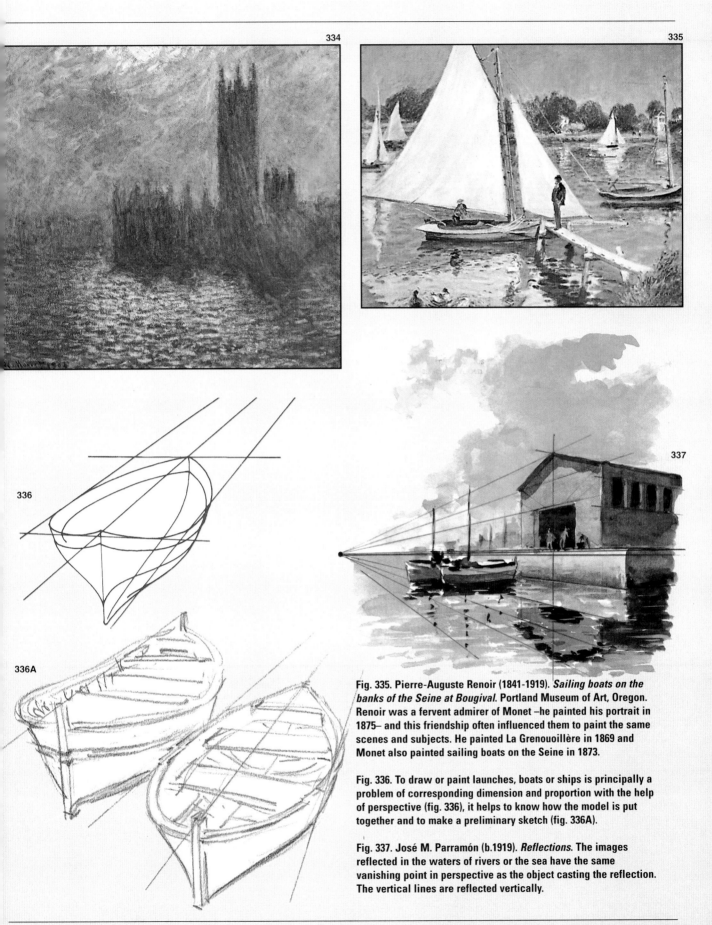

334

335

336

336A

337

Fig. 335. Pierre-Auguste Renoir (1841-1919). *Sailing boats on the banks of the Seine at Bougival.* Portland Museum of Art, Oregon. Renoir was a fervent admirer of Monet –he painted his portrait in 1875– and this friendship often influenced them to paint the same scenes and subjects. He painted La Grenouoillère in 1869 and Monet also painted sailing boats on the Seine in 1873.

Fig. 336. To draw or paint launches, boats or ships is principally a problem of corresponding dimension and proportion with the help of perspective (fig. 336), it helps to know how the model is put together and to make a preliminary sketch (fig. 336A).

Fig. 337. José M. Parramón (b.1919). *Reflections.* The images reflected in the waters of rivers or the sea have the same vanishing point in perspective as the object casting the reflection. The vertical lines are reflected vertically.

The Sea

It was in the month of June in 1888 when Van Gogh went to Saintes Maries, near Arles and painted the sea (fig. 388). He wrote to his brother Théo from there saying *"The color of the sea is constantly changing. One minute it is green, the next minute it's blue or lilac"*. Exactly. The sea, lakes or rivers take their color from the sky, reflecting it. In this painting by Van Gogh the sea and the sky are blue, if the sky is cloudy the sea will appear grayish and during a sunset the color of the sea can appear to be orange.

Van Gogh painted this painting from nature and from memory. Yes, in order to capture the waves on canvas, painting in front of the subject Van Gogh painted *from memory*. I will explain what I mean with a quote from Claude Monet, who, in a letter to his wife Alice wrote from Britain, where he was painting the sea, *"Every day I understand a little more of this rascal. She sends me mad, but I have learned that to paint the sea satisfactorily, you need to study her all day, every day, and from exactly the same viewpoint"*.

Not really surprising if you look at it this way; in order to paint the sea as Van Gogh did or as I myself did in this painting of the Costa Brava in Catalonia (fig. 339), you have to study it for a long time, look at the colors that make up the waves, the shapes and the froth of the waves, the shimmer of the glistening water. You will see that fortunately the shapes and colors repeat themselves over and over again, something that allows you to study them, commit them to memory and finally you will be able –like Monet– to paint them from memory.

In this same illustration, study the shapes and colors of the rocks. Their structure is geometrical, represented as planes of different colors in a range of cold colors, the deeper tones are used where the rocks meet the sea, the limit of the lavaves marks a line around the base of the rocks.

Look carefully at the following details:
• In accordance with the laws of contrast and atmosphere, the color of the sea and of the rocks is lighter and the contrasts not as great in the background as in the foreground.
• The white spray must be painted from memory, it appears along the dark fringes where the sea meets the rocks.
• See how the sea in the foreground is a deep blue, almost black with hints of light and shadow that give the waves shape. You have to paint it just as you see it, without the preconception that the sea is blue.

Fig. 338. Vincent van Gogh (1853-1890). *The sea at Saints Maries.* **The Pushkin Fine Arts Museum, Moscow. The sky is blue and so is the sea, but, what a sea! With this dramatic use of impasto the texture of the waves is transformed by this apparent relief.**
Fig. 339. José M. Parramón (b. 1919). *Costa Brava.* **Private collection. An example of the different techniques to capture the shapes and colors of the rocks, the spray and the sea.**

Figures in Landscape

It is not that they are indispensable, but sometimes they are necessary. In a landscape in the middle of the countryside, high in the mountains you can do without people. In an urban landscape it is both logical and necessary to include figures and cars... unless you are looking to create a special effect, something intentionally dramatic as Antonio López does with his urban landscape *Gran Vía* on page 97. You should, if possible, include figures on roadsides or on the outskirts of a village or at the beach next to the boats, and so on.

The Impressionists often included crowds of people in their paintings in a display of synthesis. I describe it as such because they described the figures, tiny figures, with three or four brushstrokes, one for a hat, another for the face, another for the shirt or jacket and the last to describe the skirt or trousers (fig. 340).

To paint figures with such ease requires a fair amont, actually a considerable amont, of practice. The figures that you see in the street, in a square or on the roadside are figures that are sometimes standing still, waiting or talking to eachother, but there will also be figures who are walking or moving around. You will have to paint them as you did the waves and the spray on the sea, from memory, by referring back to the models who, fortunately repeat their movements.

Your first step is to learn how to draw figures from images in photos, studying them for a while and drawing them afterwards from memory (figs. 341 & 342). You will have to do this exercise over and over again, first with printed images of models, later drawing and painting from life –with pens, colored pencils or wax, etc.– go to a park where you can sit down and make sketches of people sitting on benches or passers by (fig. 343).

As a summary of my comments, have a look at figures 345 to 347. Study the step by step watercolor study of various figures based on a photo (fig. 344).

Figs. 341 & 342 (opposite page). Try to get in a lot of practice drawing groups of people first in pencil, copying photos in magazines. Start by copying, then look at the photo and then put it aside and draw from memory.

Fig. 343. Go along to a park or a square one day to sketch, start with people who are still, sitting on benches or chatting to each other. Then move on to drawing or painting walking figures. You can use colored pencils, pens or wax. Go ahead, it's fun.

Figs. 344 to 347. Have a look at this figure sketch in watercolor done step by step based on the photo. This is something you can try and you will achieve results through plenty of practice.

340

Fig. 340. Camille Pissarro. *Place du Théâtre*, Paris (detail). The Hermitage Museum. St Petersburg. The quality of these figures reveals Pissarro's rapid vision and his capacity to capture and synthesise movement, shape and color.

341

342

344

343

347

345

346

Fig. 348. Vicenç Ballestar (b. 1929). *The river*. Private collection.
Ballestar is in the process of finishing a step by step watercolor
which you can see overleaf on page 144. The photo shows the
moment when Ballestar is adding depth to the soft tones of the
river, working up from the bottom with a number 18 brush applying
a mixture of ultramarine blue and burnt umber which belong to
the range of sooty, broken colors with which Ballestar has painted
this watercolor.

COLOR AND LANDSCAPE PAINTING IN PRACTICE

We are now going to talk about color, color theories
and how these theories enable us to paint all the colors
of nature with only three colors (plus white when
painting in oils). There are four more pages explaining
color harmonies in landscape and we will compare the
different approaches of tonalist and colorist painting,
then we will arrive at the practical demonstrations, step
by step painting sketches, landscapes *alla prima* and in
various sessions, both in watercolor and in oil. Finally,
all that is needed is a complete glossary of terms to
finish up this book about *painting landscapes
in oils and watercolor*.

Color Theory

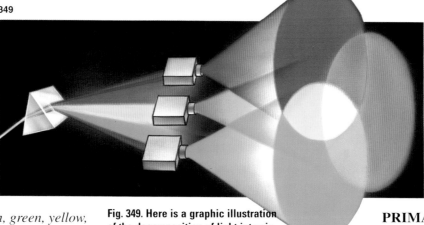

349

Light is color. Two hundred years ago the physicist Isaac Newton proved this theory. He shut himself in a darkened room, and intercepted a ray of light with a prism, he managed to *refract white light* into the six colors of the spectrum, *deep blue, cyan, green, yellow, red and magenta.*

A hundred years later another scientist, Thomas Young, studied Newton's theories, he projected the six colors of the spectrum using six lanterns and through elimination he made a seminal discovery: *With only three light colors, red, green and deep blue he could make white light, he established the primary colors of light.*

By recreating white light, Young went on to see that by mixing the three primary colors in pairs he obtained another three colors, the secondary light colors, yellow, magenta and cyan (fig. 349).

Now I need your undivided attention. Up until this moment we have been talking about light and light colors and the result of two light colors –red and green– doubles the quantity of light, giving us a brighter light; yellow (physicists call this the additive processs which, by the way is the system used for television). However, we don't paint with light. Our mixes of colors always presume loss of brightness (for the physicist amongst you, that is the subtractive process). As a result our pigment based colors are lighter and we take these colors as the basis of our spectrum.

Fig. 349. Here is a graphic illustration of the decomposition of light into six colors (Newton) and of the recomposition of light (Young) loth only three colors, the primary ones (red light, intense blue and green).

Our primary colors are the secondary light colors and vice versa, our secondary colors are primary light colors.

So, here are the artist's colors (you will see them in the diagram on the opposite page).

Figs. 354, 354A & 355. The same landscape painted with oil and watercolor using only the three primary colors; Prussian blue, madder carmine and lemon cadmium yellow (and white in the oil painting).

354A

ARTIST'S PRIMARY COLORS
(Fig. 350)
Yellow, Magenta, Cyan

If you mix these primary colors in pairs you get

SECONDARY COLORS
(Fig. 351)

Red	**(magenta & yellow)**
Green	**(blue & yellow)**
Bright Blue	**(blue & magenta)**

By mixing primary colors with secondary colors in pairs, we get

354

TERTIARY COLORS
(Fig. 352)

Light green (yellow & green)
Emerald green (green & blue)
Ultramarine blue (blue & deep blue)
Violet (deep blue & magenta)
Carmine (magenta & red)
Orange (red & yellow)

Study this chromatic wheel and you will see all these colors in order, P indicates primary colors, S indicates secondary colors and T indicates tertiary colors (fig. 353).

We have now arrived at the following important conclusion which is derived from the color theories just reviewed:

The perfect relationship between light colors and pigment colors allows us to paint all the colors that nature produces with only three colors: yellow, magenta and cyan.

Take a look at the identical landscape painted in oils and watercolor, both were painted using only three colors (and white in the oil painting) on figures 354, 354A & 355.

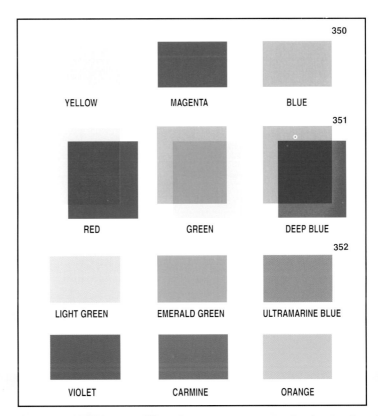

Figs. 350, 351 & 352. A graphic illustrating the pigment colors; the three primary colors (350) the three secondary colors (351) and the six tertiary colors (352). The colors correspond to those on Ostwald's wheel.
Fig. 353. The chromatic circle with the three primary colors (P), the three secondary colors (S) and the six tertiary colors (T).

355

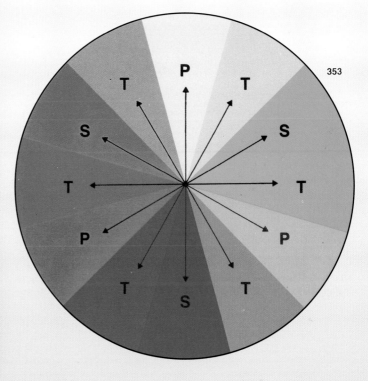

353

Complementary Colors

Figure 356, on the opposite page, is another diagram of Thomas Young's experiment with three lanterns and the beams of light colors red, green and bright blue which when projected and superimposed make up white light. In figure 357, we will see that when the beam of bright blue light is interrupted the color yellow appears. We can see that this yellow that is missing is the complementary color to the bright blue, which would be necessary to make up the white light and vice versa.

This trick of making up white light with other light colors also works with other colors of the spectrum and given that our pigment colors are made up of the same spectrum as light colors, complementary paint colors are the same, with one fundamental difference: with light colors when beams of light are superimposed the brightness increases and white light is obtained, when pigment colors are mixed they subtract from the light and black is obtained (fig. 358).

HERE ARE THE PAINT COMPLEMENTARY COLORS (Fig. 358)

Yellow is complementary to bright blue

Magenta is complementary to green

Cyan is complementary to red

Look at the diagram below (fig. 359) this is a chromatic circle with the complementary colors situated opposite eachother.

To what effect can we use these complementary colors? In the first place to obtain the maximum color contrast by juxtaposing the two colors (fig. 360). Secondly, in order to paint with a range of broken colors which are made by mixing complementary colors in unequal amounts, and adding white when using oils (figs. 361 & 361A).

Fig. 359. The chromatic wheel with the complementary colors situated opposite eachother.

Fig. 360. Maurice Denis (1870-1943). *Westminster Bridge.* **Private collection, Paris. You can see in this fauve painting how Denis has used the complementary colors, applying them to attain very bold contrasts.**

360

359

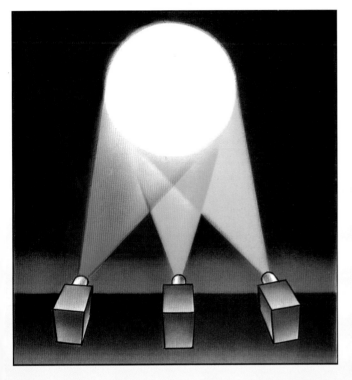

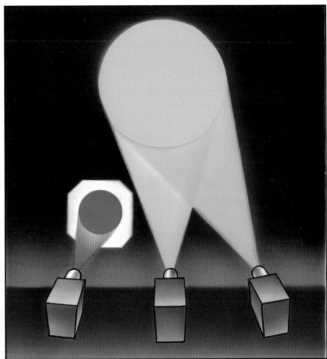

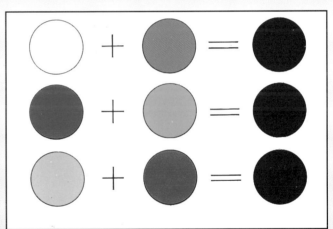

Figs. 361A & B. The creation of white light with three of Young's lanterns (fig. 356), by interrupting the beam of red light (fig. 357) you can see that red is the complementary color to bright blue.

Fig. 361C. This diagram shows how the combination of complementary pigment colors makes black.

Fig. 361D & E. Josep Ayneto, *Urban scene*. Private collection. Ayneto has painted this watercolor landscape with a range of broken colors, the product of mixing unequal amonts of two complementary colors and white (in this case the white of the paper (fig. 361A).

Color Harmonies and Color Ranges

Harmonizing color is nothing more than interpreting the picture using a particular range of colors. This practice is evident when you study the works of the great masters, Rubens for example painted with siennas, reds and yellows using a *warm color range*, and Velázquez painted his figures with a *broken color range*; browns and grays. The landscapes painted by the impressionists are dominated by the *cold color range*. Fortunately, Nature always provides us with perfect color ranges and light to appreciate them by. In the bright sunlight of a summer's day or at sunset the light tends to be warm; yellows, ochres and siennas dominate (fig. 362). With the same amount of light, in the middle of winter, or early in the morning the landscape is dominated by cold colors; by blues and greens (fig. 363). And on a cloudy or rainy day the colors tend towards gray and the range of gray sooty colors, broken colors (fig. 364). Whatever the case you can accentuate these variations, even to the point of changing the dominant color range you observe in the model, allowing you to interpret it more freely. Have a look at the three examples of the different landscapes, each with a specific color range harmonizing the landscape.

362

363

364

Figs. 362, 363, & 364 (photos by José M. Parramón). These photos were taken of places that I painted. They were taken at different times of day, the first two are in bright sunlight, the lower one taken when it was fairly overcast. They demonstrate that Nature harmonizes colors with a tendency towards a warm, cold or broken range of colors.

365

365A

Warm color range (fig. 365). This consists of reds and colors related to red including greenish yellow, yellow, orange, red, carmine, purple and violet. See the colors on the chromatic circle (fig. 365A). The appearance of occasional cold colors such as blue or green doesn't detract from the dominant warm color range of the painting.

Cold color range (fig. 366). This range is made up of blues and colors related to blue, look at the chromatic circle (fig. 366A) and you will see greenish yellow, green, emerald green, cyan, ultramarine blue, dark blue and violet. As with the other color ranges, the occasional color from another range i.e. warm colors can appear within this dominantly cold range of colors.

366

366A

Broken color range (fig. 367). This is the color range preferred by many artists because of its chromatic qualities, resulting from an unequal mix of complementary colors, softened with white paint if using oils or the white of the paper when painting watercolors (fig. 367A). A rànge which offers a warm, cold or even neutral selection of colors, often with impressive results.

367A

Figs. 365, 366 & 367 (from the top downwards). José M. Parramón (b. 1919). *Wheat field with Breda in the background*. Private collection (fig. 365). This landscape in oils was painted using a range of warm colors. *The farmhouse*. Private collection (fig. 366). Landscape painted in oils using a cold range of colors. *Refuge hut high in the mountains*. Private collection. (fig. 367) Watercolor painted with a broken range of colors. Next to each picture is a chromatic wheel showing the warm and cold color ranges and lastly the use of complementary colors in this image.

367

137

Tonalist Landscape, Colorist Landscape

André Lhote (1885-1962) a French professor, artist and author of a number of books including *A Treatise on Landscape and Figure Painting*, distinguishes in his book between the two great traditions of landscape which he defines as:

A: The Colorists. Those who value first and foremost the use of color.

B: The Tonalists. Those who prefer to interpret through the interplay of light and shadow.

The Tonalists have always existed, since the time of the Greek artists; Apelles, Zeuxis, etc., 500 years B. C. up until artists of the twentieth century such as Dalí (fig. 368). Tonalists describe forms using tonal values, shaping objects with light and shade. The first colorists worked in the Gothic period, they were the manuscript illuminators. Through the following centuries there were few artists that could be described as colorists until the time of the Impressionists and Post-Impressionists. Van Gogh is a clear example of a colorist painter (fig. 369). All artists who describe shapes with flat planes of color, not using shadows, believe that *color itself provides diversity, it distinguishes and explains the shape of objects.* It remains to be said that landscapes painted in a colorist manner are much closer to a modern approach to painting and, don't forget that *to paint using a colorist approach, front lighting is the most suitable as it tends to minimise the shadows, diffuse light is also effective, i.e. light conditions of a cloudy day.*

Inevitably however, there are exceptions. I painted the image overleaf (fig. 370) a little while ago, a side view of the Barcelona cathedral lit from behind, with a tonalist approach, and I have painted this copy as an exercise and demonstration for you to see the same picture but in a colorist style with a brief step by step explanation which will allow you to follow the process (figs. 371, 372 & 373).

368

369

370

Fig. 370. José M. Parramón (b. 1919). *The Cathedral quarter, Barcelona*. Private collection. A totally tonalist interpretation with backlighting, painted in oils from nature.

Fig. 371. This is the first step of the transformation of the initial painting into a colorist painting. I started by making a charcoal drawing, then using oils I painted the sky and clouds very much as before but introducing pinkish tones.

Fig. 372. Paint the part which in the original stays covered in the shadow of the silhouette, but keeping to the Fauve style, close to colorism: painting this shady part in a range of blues that create a colorful luminosity.

371

Fig. 368 (opposite page). Salvador Dalí (1904-1984). *Back view of Dalí painting a back view of Gala*. Fundación Gala-Salvador Dalí, Figueras. In both his surrealist paintings and his realist paintings Salvador Dalí was always a tonalist painter, a satisfying explanation of how the volume of the figures is created through the observation of light and shadow.

Fig. 369 (opposite page). Vincent van Gogh (1853-1890). *Les Alyscamps*. Private collection, Lausanne. Van Gogh, a one hundred percent colorist painter, made three studies of this avenue, each in flat colors and doing away with any expression of light and shade that is a characteristic of tonalist painting.

372

373

Fig. 373. I continue with a fauvist-colorist interpretation in mind, adding the light effects of the backlighting with yellows, oranges and reds, in contrast to the part in shadow, painted with blues, greens and violets. I have created an image in which the interplay of light and shade is evident but the brightness and contrasts are expressed in a colorist manner.

Ballestar Paints a Study in Watercolor

The painting of a study, whether it is in watercolor or oils, can often be a picture or exercise that gives rise to a larger work, sometimes however, it is a work in its own right. Whichever the case, in a study three aspects should be born in mind: *paint swiftly, paint with full concentration and paint spontaneously.* This is especially important in this study painted by my colleague Vicenç Ballestar in which the sky and the stormy clouds are the focus of the work.

Ballestar starts this study by drawing with charcoal, which is then dusted off with a clean cloth leaving faint traces which will serve as guidelines when he paints. It is simply a schematic *line drawing* (fig. 374). He starts painting by wetting the entire sheet of paper with clean water using a wide synthetic brush of 4 cm.

He waits until the paper has absorbed the excess water and prepares a mixture of colors to paint the clouds with ultramarine blue, burnt Sienna and Van Dyck brown, which combine to make up a dark gray which he uses to start painting the top part of the sky. You can see the process step by step in figures 375 to 380. Ballestar paints very rapidly and with absolute concentration, adding and removing color, absorbing a little here and there, opening white spaces (as you can see in fig. 380).

He then goes straight on to paint the trees with Hooker green, olive green and permanent green, resolving the strip of land with a wash of burnt Sienna and ultramarine blue (figs. 381 & 382). Finally he decides to strengthen the sky colors, adding and extending the color towards the right (fig. 383). A few finishing touches on the strip of land with the trees... and he signs it (fig. 384).

374 375 376 377 378 379

380

381

383

382

384

Figs. 374 to 380 (opposite page). In figure 374, Ballestar makes a line drawing of the subject in charcoal which he then partially rubs out with a cloth. Next he wets the area where the sky is to be painted and while waiting for the surface to dry a little, he makes up a color to paint the clouds with ultramarine blue, burnt Sienna and Van Dyck brown, you only need to study the following images 375 to 380 to see how Ballestar has applied color onto the tilted support, first with a 4 cm brush and then with a 1 cm brush, adding and absorbing excess paint. He paints the sky, which is nearly finished in figure 380.

Figs. 381 & 382 (above). He now paints the trees using Hooker green, olive green, and permanent green; and finishes the strip of land with burnt Sienna with a touch of ultramarine blue.

Figs. 383 & 384. As a finishing touch I asked him to reinforce the colors of the stormy sky. He does this and finally finishes off by strengthening the color of the trees along the strip of land.

Painting a Study in Oils

I painted this picture on a number 8 landscape canvas (46 cm x 33 cm), keeping in mind the three key points mentioned before: paint swiftly, concentrate and be spontaneous.

I started the picture by tracing a vertical and a horizontal line, forming a cross on the canvas, to facilitate the calculation of dimensions and proportions (fig. 385). I started by painting the sky with its cumulus clouds, introducing a blue color made up of ultramarine and cobalt blue, white and a touch of carmine. Then I launched myself into painting the mountain on the left, using thick, flat brush strokes with a number 10 or 12 brush (fig. 386). Next, I painted the mountain on the right with its patches of earth and pinkish rocks, I covered the group of poplars with dark gray using plenty of turps and added in the bright green field in the foreground (fig. 387).

The fourth phase was a transitional one, I filled the gaps and rounded off details before the final touches (fig. 388).

And here is the finished article (fig. 389), strengthening the color of the sky and clouds, altering the green of the field by introducing a layer of bluer green, painting in the poplars, adding the line of green trees on the left and the grass and the two bare trees in the foreground.

Fig. 386. I paint the sky with its cumulus clouds, detail the mountains on the left and in the background with prussian blue, carmine, burnt Sienna and white, trying to fill out the white areas to avoid the problem of simultaneous contrasts.

Fig. 387. There is an interplay of colors on the mountain to the right, its crested by a permanent green mixed with blue and ochre, just below this is strip of white, carmine and vermilion. Below this pinkish strip I introduce a dark grayish area and at the base of the mountain on the left I introduce the same gray with a little blue and burnt umber, with plenty of turps so that it dries quickly. Finally I paint the field with blue, greenish yellow and white.

385

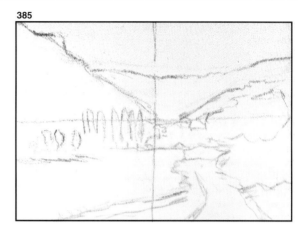

Fig. 385. With charcoal I draw a vertical and a horizontal line which cross the canvas providing a guideline for calculating dimensions and proportions. I check, for example, that the diagonals of the two mountains on either side coincide in the center. I use fixer on the the charcoal sketch.

386

387

Fig. 388. I fill up the white spaces –the road and the dark zone beneath the mountain on the right.

Fig. 389. Here is the final result, with a general retouch of the sky and the clouds, painting the white poplars on top of the dark background, the trees on the left, the road and the tufts of grass in the foreground. I touch up the green of the field in the foreground with a layer of bluer green and last I add the two bare trees into the foreground on the right.

388

389

Ballestar Paints a Landscape in Watercolor (I)

My colleague Ballestar is left handed. It is for this reason that he paints with his paintbox on the left next to a container of water (it is his palette that is on page 43, fig. 80). On his right he has a piece of cloth with which he rubs, cleans and dries off the water and pigment from the brush (varying how hard he rubs the brush depending on whether he is absorbing excess color, just a little or a lot), using a large or small brush, for softening the color on wetted areas or lifting off white spaces, all of which we'll see as he paints this watercolor. Ballestar uses two synthetic brushes; a 4 cm brush and a smaller one, 1 or 2 cm, and two sable brushes, a number 8 and a finer number 6 brush.

This is an accomplished watercolor don't you think? Look at it in its nearly finished state (fig. 397). This watercolor has been painted in a delicate range of broken colors... the subject is appealing: a river flowing between steep banks on a cloudy day... Ballestar said to me: "When I saw the scene I was reminded of Monet's paintings and his time at Giverny, when he painted the Seine series and the snow. Do you remember?". Yes, of course.

Look at figure 390, Ballestar's drawing in charcoal: just a few lines that he half deletes using a clean cloth afterwards, leaving a faint trace as a guideline.

He now turns to the banks either side of the river and paints them using a number 8 sable brush, alternating it with a synthetic brush 1 or 2 cm wide (figs. 393 & 394), he continues working only with this palette of broken colors, made up of cobalt blue and ultramarine blue and, to make it grayer at certain points he uses Van Dyck brown. He also adds a hint of violet in those same areas –look at the left bank– to liven the gray tones. He even uses a touch of broken vermilion on the right bank to break the

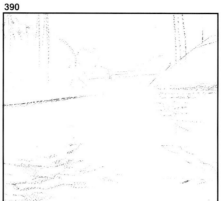

Figs. 390, 391 & 392. First he makes a simple line drawing of the subject, then Ballestar goes on to wet the Fontenay de Canson paper, he waits a moment, tests the wetness of the paper and with a 4 cm brush he applies a delicate wash in the sky which becomes deeper in color as he works down the paper to the waters of the river.

Figs. 393, 394 & 395. He immediately starts painting the two banks, outlining the details including the reflections of the banks in the water. He achieves this using the technique of painting wet on wet, alternating with applying dry, using a sable number 8 brush and a synthetic 2 cm brush.

monotony of the subdued color range. Look at the way that in the shadows he accentuates the ultramarine blue so that this blue stands out in the color mix of the wet on wet patches. The demands of this technique, which depends on the wetness of the paper, mean that Ballestar paints an area, maybe he wipes his brush on a cloth and then moves on to another area, only to return again to the patch he resolved earlier, cleaning and wiping the brush again. He is taking the advice of Ingres who recommended that his pupils *"paint everything at once, paint it all at once, as if the entire image progresses and improves until it is finished"*. Wet, dry, painting wet on wet, cleaning the brush absorbing excess paint with a cloth... painting dry and... alternating these techniques, seeing when he needs to give patches of paper time to dry, working meanwhile on other areas that are already dry enough. With this constant animation, incessant use of the cloth, Ballestar practically finishes the banks on either side, deepens the gray of the river in the foreground (figs. 395 & 396) and arrives at the end of this first phase, now there are only a few final touches to apply and the painting will be finished (fig. 397).

395

Figs. 396 & 397. He works adding details to the bank on the right and adds in some reflections of both banks, so that looking at the image below (fig. 397) the watercolor could be seen as finished.

396

397

Ballestar Paints a Landscape in Watercolor (II)

398

399

400

401

When we talked about finishing this picture (fig. 397 overleaf) we said that there were only a few details to add before it would be ready to sign. That is certainly the case, have a look at the first image on this page (fig. 398). Ballestar has described the shape and colors of the trees on the extreme right of the painting, using a number 6 sable brush to paint them in on the bank.

He speeds up the drying process of the paint on the left bank by using a hairdryer –a tool often used by professional watercolorists– so that the surface is dry and ready to apply some shadows (fig. 399) and then he takes up a narrow 1 or 2 cm brush and works with it on its side, adding horizontal brushstrokes to represent the reflections in the middle ground (fig. 400). With the same brush he adds further reflections in the middle ground (fig. 401) and opens some lighter spaces by reabsorbing the color to represent the reflections of the trees on the right bank (fig. 402). Ballestar takes a step back from his task finishing the picture, contemplating it for a while, he considers it from a distance and decides that the coloring on the water, which is darker in the foreground and lighter in the middle ground, is still not as he wants it, "Of course I am not aiming for a blend of color as if it were applied with an airbrush, but..." he commented, and without a second thought he takes up the hairdryer and makes sure that the paint of the river is entirely dry. Putting down the hairdryer he takes up a wide 4 cm brush and with a little gray he adds a few horizontal strokes to the river water (fig. 403) until he has achieved what he was looking for. You can see the finished watercolor in figure 404. Good work Ballestar my friend!

Figs. 398 to 404. All the images on these two pages form part of a finishing process, and as we can see in figure 398, Ballestar finishes the trees on the right bank, in figure 399 he uses a hairdryer to speed up the drying process, in figure 400 he adds further touches to the reflections. You will notice in all these pictures how Ballestar holds the brush quite a long way up the stem. In figure 401 he continues working on the reflections and in figure 402 he is opening white spaces, vertical lines with a 1 or 2 cm brush. Finally in figure 403 he subtly strengthens the color of the water and figure 404 shows the final work, signed by Ballestar.

A Colorist Landscape in Oils (I)

You can see the subject of this landscape in figure 412 (opposite page), it is a little mountain village, situated at the foot of a mountain range, with a row of trees in the foreground. It is also evident that I have painted this landscape using a colorist approach, quite fauvist, a style defined, as you may remember, by Othon Friesz, when he said: *"Capturing the sun's brilliance, the technique is based on combining colors with the passion and emotion aroused by nature"*.

Indeed, I can affirm that I felt this passion and emotion while I was drawing and painting, while keeping two points in mind: First, I must paint in the large open white spaces, covering over the white canvas to avoid the negative effect of the law of simultaneous contrasts, and second, I must follow Corot's advice:

"It is crucial to paint an overall scene at the first try. All that you paint straight from nature will appear more natural and whatsmore you can count on serendipity".

I use a number 15 figure canvas (65 x 54), using mostly thick hogshair brushes, both flat and filbert, numbers 12, 14 & 16. I start by making a drawing in charcoal, tracing a vertical and a horizontal line which intersect in the center, this is to make the calculation of dimensions and proportions easier. I fix the drawing and start painting the sky with madder carmine, white and Prussian blue, I then move on to the mountains in the background with Prussian blue and white (fig. 405).

I then start working on the mountains to the left and right (figs. 406 & 407) –I am trying to eliminate large areas of white on the canvas– working at first on the overall impression from "top to bottom", as Corot advised, trying to interpret the huge diversity of colors that appear in this mountain scene in a colorist fashion.

405

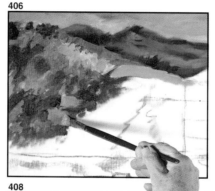
406

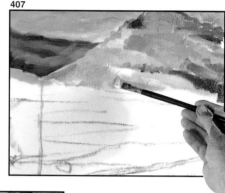
407

408

Fig. 405. I start with a sketch in charcoal and trace a cross, lining up the profile of the mountains so that the vertical line cuts through the center and the group of houses is sketched in below the horizontal line. I spray the drawing with fixer and paint the sky and the mountains in the background.

409

I am now going to paint the terraced fields in the center of the scene (fig. 408). Look at the contrasts that I have exaggerated in the lower section, to make the colors stand out and give volume to the houses. I am using plenty of turps with the paint so that tomorrow when the paint is somewhat drier I can continue painting and touching up the colors, adding lines, shadows and highlights, etc.

Next, I paint in the line of trees in the foreground (fig. 409), first with a layer of light green, then I work on the light and shadow, with emerald green and carmine, adding a touch of prussian blue here and there and the highlights which are painted using emerald green, ochre and a hint of white, raw Sienna and yellow. Finally I paint the roofs (fig. 410), the shadows cast by the roofs (fig. 411) and then I leave it to finish tomorrow.

410

411

Figs. 406 & 407. I paint the mountains on the right and left with a wide range of colors, basically a mixture of prussian blue, a little burnt umber, permanent green, ochre, madder carmine. I have added white to these colors in certain places.

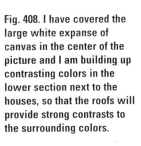

Fig. 408. I have covered the large white expanse of canvas in the center of the picture and I am building up contrasting colors in the lower section next to the houses, so that the roofs will provide strong contrasts to the surrounding colors.

Figs. 409 & 410. I add in the line of trees in the foreground, and leave them as finished. I work on the roofs of the houses and the shadows projected by them and add the two triangles of grassland in the immediate foreground.

Figs. 411 & 412. Last I work on the color of the houses' facades in the foreground (fig. 411) and reach the end of the first stage of the painting, and I think about how I will continue with it tomorrow (see the following page).

412

A Colorist Landscape in Oils (II)

It was yesterday morning, 24 hours ago that I left off painting, so that I could continue with it today. It is not dry, but it now has bite, a firm enough surface so that I can over-paint to retouch and alter certain colors. Look at the mountain on the left for example, if you compare it with how it looked yesterday (fig. 413) and how it looks now (fig. 414), see how the alterations higher up in the center have been made using different shapes and colors; and look on the left of the bank of yellow ochre, overpainted again to change the shapes and colors. Now look at the area just above the houses and you'll see quite a development, the trees and the colors behind the houses have been altered to create a stronger color contrast with the roofs.

You can see these alterations of color in figures 415 & 416, the stepped fields are now brightened with more intense greens, a mix of emerald green and permanent green with ochres, reds, blues, violet made up of ultramarine blue and carmine, etc. If you study figure 416, the bushes and small trees are already detailed, so are the lines indicating the different levels of the fields.

Finally, in figure 417, I have painted the openings and windows of the houses with a flat number 4 sable brush, using a mixture of ultramarine blue, emerald green and carmine, each window a single brushstroke. In figure 417, you can also see the other brushes that I have at hand, one with cream paint and another with white, for retouching inadvertent smudges of black paint.

Figure 418 shows the final result, after the finishing touches such as

the addition of green blinds to many of the windows, touching up of the colors of some of the roofs, etc. So now this colorist painting, which I have worked on from "top to bottom" as Corot advised, is truly finished.

Figs. 413 to 418. The following day the paint is not too fresh and has dried enough for me to continue painting, touching up and finishing off the details as follows: I re-painted the mountainside on the left as you can see by comparing figure 414 with 413, I painted and added to the areas to the left and right of the central area (figs. 415 & 416) and I painted the windows of the houses, retouching the colors and outlines of the facades (fig. 417) and stepping back to see the final result in figure 418.

417

418

Composition and Interpretation of a Landscape (I)

So, here I am on the planes of Castilla, looking over this landscape from a promontory (fig. 419). I set up the easel a while ago, I have chosen a canvas, number 10 portrait, 55 cm x 46 cm and the colors are laid out on the palette. But, I'm still not painting. I am preparing, studying and looking a the subject, attempting to see it my way, imagining and combining images, analyzing the possibilities, bringing other images, paintings and photos to mind and imagining possible alterations...

Suddenly I switch the horizontal position of the canvas to vertical. Now I imagine that I am higher up, looking at the scene from a more elevated viewpoint, the perspective allows me to separate out the further planes. I also imagine myself narrowing my field of vision, conceiving of this compositional format that you can see in figures 420 and 421.

Using this format I draw the landscape in charcoal including all the light and shadows, attempting to see it expressed as forms which at this time are nothing more than concepts. The problem of dimensions and proportions easily resolves itself thanks to the division of the foreground into horizontal and diagonal planes. As part of my interpretation of the scene I have made the hay bales in the foreground bigger, placing them in a pattern that accentuates the perspective of the foreground (fig. 422). However, if you compare the drawing with the original you will see that the spacing, the trees and the fields are practically the same.

I spray the drawing with fixer and now at last I am ready to paint.

I mix the colors for the sky and the hills in the background with white, vermilion, a touch of ultramarine blue, an even smaller hint of Van Dyck brown, for the sky; and for the mountains, a mix of burnt sienna and ultramarine blue with a touch of white to make the color grayer, and

419

420

421

422

Figs. 419, 420 & 421. The subject, figure 419, is a plain consisting of cornfields and scrubland in the foreground and grassy fields with trees and a range of mountains in the background. I am imagining a higher point of vision, so I can separate each plane and I imagine it in a vertical format, like the study in figure 420 and the preparatory sketch in figure 421.

Fig. 422. I draw the landscape with charcoal, making an assertive interpretation of the scene, adding in the shapes, tones and interplay of light and shade to the sketch.

423

424

as I mix these colors I remember Corot's advice, about painting from top to bottom, step by step,

"... in the most comprehensive way possible, from the first attempt, in such a way that there is very little to add when you have finished".

So, I start by painting the sky and the mountains, using vermilion and carmine with a touch of white as a basis for the colors (fig. 423).
Next I paint the cypresses and fields in the background, and as I do so a thought of Cézanne's comes to mind, a thought that any painter of oils or watercolors should remember and always bear in mind. Cézanne said:

"You could say that TO PAINT IS TO CONTRAST".

This is demonstrated right here, I want the cypresses in the background to look darker so that they stand out better, so I lighten the colors that frame them and then I move on to paint the green field and another line of trees in the background (fig. 424).
In the next pictures, figures 425 & 426, I have restructured the area on the right, redrawing the mountains with the paints, using a veil of Prussian blue, madder carmine, a little Van Dyck brown and a touch of white.
Now look at figure 427, the painting has progressed in this first step, the top third is now almost finished.

Figs. 423 and 424. Paint the sky and the mountains last and, in the following figure, finish the lawn, the trees, and the cypresses, brightening the rosy pink shade underneath to enhance the contrast.

425

426

427

Figs. 425, 426, & 427. I draw and paint the right side of the background, first adding dashes of color and then strengthening it. I then alter the colors by adding a veil of Prussian blue to the mountains.

Composition and Interpretation of a Landscape (II)

428

I continue painting "from top to bottom" and develop the line of trees on the right. I identify the green of the fields as a mixture of emerald green, a little carmine, a touch of ochre and white. By adding more carmine and some prussian blue to the mixture I create a dark green, almost black, for the line of trees. With emerald green, carmine, ochre and white I produce the light green for the highlighted areas. Then, for the autumnal tree at the end of the line on the left, I have mixed madder carmine with a little emerald green, vermilion and burnt umber, using a little ochre for the highlights (fig. 428).

It has been bothering me ever since I started to paint that there is a lot of white space, glaring white of the canvas still without paint. This is the moment to fill in those gaps with colors even if they are rough approximations of color, so that the dangers of blank canvas are avoided. As you already know, there is a risk that you can miscalculate colors and tones because of simultaneous contrasts. So I rapidly paint the wheat field in the middle ground (fig. 429), the green triangular field and the yellow ochre field with its straw bales that cuts diagonally across the foreground (fig. 430).

429

430

Fig. 428. I paint the line of trees in the middle ground including a tree with autumnal colors, I alter the color of the mountains in the background, returning back to the original colors.

Fig. 429 & 430. I decide to "fill in the white spaces", painting the fields of corn with a yellow ochre mixed with white and the triangular grass sward in green, the colors are not yet accurate but they serve to cover the disconcerting white spaces of the canvas.

Fig. 431. Next I paint the line of trees in the middle ground adding the interplay of light and shadows and...

431

Next I start work on the line of trees in the wheat field across the middle ground (fig. 431) and I paint in the triangular piece of uncultivated land in the foreground. In real life it is a reddish sienna color, however, I am going to interpret the area with very little definition, without including the little bushes of dried plants which you can see in the original. So instead I paint the background a dark color and leave shapes undefined, just including little hints of light and shade (fig. 432) leaving it to finish later with a lighter color in the same broken range (fig. 433), to suggest the bushes and grasses in an indefinite way... something that helps to create the illusion of depth (remember the formula on page 98 that the English landscape painters used at the end of the eighteenth century, that the French painter Rousseau commented on, concerning how an indefinite and unfocused foreground can be painted to create depth). You can see in figure 433, the final step of this stage, with the mountains back to their original color, having decided that the grayish colors are indeed better than the stronger blue I added earlier.

Figs. 432 & 433 ... and I finish off the foreground of rough ground covered in scrub, first by painting it with dark gray using plenty of turps (fig. 432), and then adding a covering of sketchy scrub plants over the top of this layer, in a lighter gray (fig. 433). You can see how the picture has progressed in this second phase.

Composition and Interpretation of a Landscape (III)

434

The picture has now reached its final phase, there are only a few finishing touches to be added as well as adjusting certain colors and accentuating some of the contrasts.

I am going to start by adding highlights and shadows to the straw bales and intensifying the color of the green triangle in the middle ground (fig. 434).

I alter the colors on the straw bales and add the cords that bind them up (fig. 435).

Next I add in the diagonal line of the bank separating the wheat field in the foreground and the green triangular field of grass, then I intensify the dark green horizontal line which divides the two parts of the field (fig. 436).

Finally I include the hints of color that give variety to the diagonal wheat field in the foreground (figure 437).

So, that's it? No. I have placed the canvas with its face to the wall for a couple of days so that I can then consider it with a more critical eye. I then retouched certain details; colors and contrasts in the fields and in the crowns of the trees, including adding a tree on the left and over-painting another in the middle ground on the right in autumnal colors. I have also altered the field with the straw bales once more (fig. 438). Finally I sign the painting, hoping as I do so that this painting and all the other examples in this book will help and inspire you to improve your landscape painting.

435

436

437

Figs. 434 a 438. If you compare this image with that in the last page (fig. 433) you will see that the differences are very slight, apart from the fact that the straw bales in the foreground are not finished. There are some minor changes in figure 434 such as the inclusion of a small tree in the middle ground on the right, the intensification in color of the green triangular field that separates the two yellow fields, the addition of shadows to the two trees in the row in the middle ground, some light touches of green to the scrub in the foreground, etc. In this final phase it is all a question of hints and tiny details which perfect the picture. In figure 435 I touch up the straw bales, then in figure 436 I darken the green triangle and paint a series of small vertical strokes to represent the grass, and paint the thin strip that separates the green from the yellow. In figure 437 I add some different shades of color to the field with the straw bales in the foreground. Last, but not least, the final result in figure 438, having left it for two days without looking at it, I then added little details, final dabs of paint here and there.

438

Glossary

A

Asymmetry. When we find ourselves before a painting whose composition has an intuitive structural arrangement which does not adhere to the norms or rules but which, nevertheless maintains an equilibrium of the objects featured, we are admiring an example of asymmetry.

Atmosphere. Is visible in landscape and seascape, particularly when the scene is lit from behind. It often appears that the air between the foreground and the background transforms the appearance through a succession of veil-like misty layers which create a contrast between the colors in the foreground and the softening of colors and outlines in the background. It was Leonardo da Vinci who discovered and applied atmospheric effect in his paintings.

B

Binders. Liquid substances which are used to bind powdered pigment. Pigments for oil paint are bound with viscous oil, ether, resin, balsam or wax. Watercolor pigments are bound with water and gum Arabic as well as glycerine, honey and preservative.

Bite. When a layer of oil paint is almost dry and slightly sticky it is in the right state to paint over. Even though the brush may stick slightly the artist rubs the paint over the layer below, this gives the work an attractive finish.

Broken colors (or split colors) a range of colors made up by mixing two or more complementary colors in unequal proportions (plus white if painting with oils).

C

Chiaroscuro. Rembrandt is the undisputed master of *chiaroscuro*. His paintings often feature areas where the forms and colors are discernible despite being cast in deep shadow. In his educational books Parramón always describes this as "The Art of painting light in shadows".

Color, complementary, When two primary pigment colors are mixed (yellow and cyan for example), a secondary pigment color is formed (green). This green is the complementary color to the primary color that was not included when it was mixed (purple/magenta). If you paint a strip of green and juxtapose it with a strip of purple the most dramatic contrast will be obtained. If you mix two complementary colors in unequal proportions (plus white for oil painting) a **broken color range** will be obtained.

Color, local. Is the red of a plum, the yellow of a lemon, the color of a flower. The real color of an object when it is unaltered by shadows or reflections.

Color, reflected. Color cast on an object as a result of direct or indirect reflection of light and color emanating from another object.

Color, tonal. The color found in the shadow of an object.

Colorists. Van Gogh, Matisse and the Fauves were the instigators of a colorist movement which considers color more important than the volume produced by shadows. They painted only with color and did not use shading to describe the shape of forms. This approach is evident in contemporary painting.

Cyan. Is one of the primary pigment colors of the spectrum. It is a neutral blue, equivalent of Prussian blue (toned down with white when painting with oils). The color with the name of cyan blue, is now in color charts, both as an oil paint and a watercolor paint.

D

Dippers. Metal tray with one or two small containers and a clip on the base for fixing it to the palette, used in oil painting to hold linseed oil or turps, or both if there are two containers on the tray.

Direct painting. A technique of painting called *alla prima* in Italian and *au premier coup* in French. This means to paint in one session, by painting rapidly and not turning back to rectify details.

F

Filbert. A term used to describe the rounded end of a brush, also known as **cat's tongue**.

Frame. Frames or wooden stretchers covered with canvas for oil painting, are available in certain sizes following an international table of measurements and in three different proportional measurements, landscape, marine and portrait. A stretcher can also be used by watercolor painters to mount and hold taut the paper once it is wet.

Frottage (scrubbing). Term derived from the French verb *frotter* (to rub), this is a painting technique that consists of lightly loading the brush with thick paint and scrubbing on top of an area that has already been painted and is dry or almost dry. When painting in watercolor, frottage is the same as **dry brush technique**, which consists of rubbing the brush with only a little paint over thick grain paper.

I

Impasto. Painting with thick oil paint, applying a considerable amont to the canvas, straight from the tube. The paint stands out in relief on the canvas.

L

Linseed oil. Used as a thinner in oil painting, it is a thick oil extracted from linseeds. It is usually mixed with turps.

Liquid rubber for masking. Latex liquid is used in watercolor painting to reserve small areas of white. It is visible when applied as it has a subtle colorant added, the substance resists water when painted over and can be removed by rubbing with a finger or with an eraser once the painting is dry. It is better to avoid using sable or ox hair brushes to apply liquid rubber, synthetic brushes are hardier. Wash the brush directly after use.

M

Malleable eraser. An eraser made of a plasticine type material which allows it to be molded into